A FIREFLY BOOK

Published by Firefly Books Ltd. 2016

First printing

Publisher Cataloging-in-Publication Data (U.S.)
Names: Claybourne, Anna, author.
Title: Sharks : predators of the sea / Anna Claybourne.
Description: Richmond Hill, Ontario, Canada : Firefly Books, 2016. | Includes index. | Summary: "Sharks come in many shapes and sizes and boast many unique talents, this book is a guide for children to learn all about the sharks of the deep, from sensory abilities to diet and habits" — Provided by publisher.
Identifiers: ISBN 978-1-77085-739-1 (pbk.)
Subjects: LCSH: Sharks — Juvenile literature.
Classification: LCC QL638.9C639 | DDC 597.3 – dc23

Library and Archives Canada Cataloguing in Publication
Claybourne, Anna, author
        Sharks : predators of the sea / Anna Claybourne. — First edition.
Includes index.
ISBN 978-1-77085-739-1 (paperback)
        1. Sharks—Juvenile literature. I. Title.
QL638.9.C54 2016   j597.3   C2015-908664-7

Published in the United States by
Firefly Books (U.S.) Inc.
P.O. Box 1338, Ellicott Station
Buffalo, New York 14205

Published in Canada by
Firefly Books Ltd.
50 Staples Avenue, Unit 1
Richmond Hill, Ontario L4B 0A7

Printed and bound in China

Conceived, designed, and produced by
Marshall Editions, Part of The Quarto
Group, The Old Brewery, 6 Blundell
Street, London N7 9BH

Publisher: Maxime Boucknooghe
Editorial Director: Laura Knowles
Art Director: Susi Martin
Edited, designed and picture
researched by: Starry Dog Books Ltd
Consultant: Michael Bright

SHARKS
PREDATORS OF THE SEA

ANNA CLAYBOURNE

FIREFLY BOOKS

CONTENTS

WORLD OF SHARKS 6

GREAT WHITE SHARK 8

GREAT HAMMERHEAD SHARK 10

BULL SHARK 12

SHARK TEETH 14

MAKO SHARKS 16

BLUE SHARK 18

THRESHER SHARKS 20

SHARK SKELETONS 22

SHARK SKIN 24

TIGER SHARK 26

LEMON SHARK 28

GOBLIN SHARK 30

SHARK SENSES 32

SIXTH SENSE 34

WOBBEGONG SHARKS 36

LANTERNSHARKS 38

COOKIECUTTER SHARK 40

GREENLAND SHARK 42

SHARK EGGS 44

SHARK BABIES 46

WHALE SHARK 48

MEGAMOUTH SHARK 50

FRILLED SHARK 52

REEF SHARKS 54

SHARK STORIES 56

SHARK ATTACKS 58

SHARK RELATIVES 60

MANTA RAY 62

STINGRAYS 64

ELECTRIC RAYS 66

SAWFISH 68

PREHISTORIC SHARKS 70

SHARKS IN DANGER 72

SHARK SIZES 74

GLOSSARY 76

INDEX 78

ACKNOWLEDGMENTS...80

WORLD OF SHARKS

Sharks are a type of fish. Like other fish, they have gills and breathe underwater, and they swim using their tails and fins. But they aren't just any old fish! All sharks are carnivores, and they include some of the fiercest, fastest, biggest, and strangest fish in the world. However, although sharks might seem scary, shark attacks on people are actually very rare.

AMAZING SHARKS

Sharks really are amazing! There are sharks that light up, sharks with hammer-shaped heads, and sharks that look like carpets! In this book, besides well-known sharks such as the great white, you'll meet all kinds of bizarre and beautiful sharks that you might not have known about before.

Shark features
Many sharks have muscular, torpedo-shaped bodies.

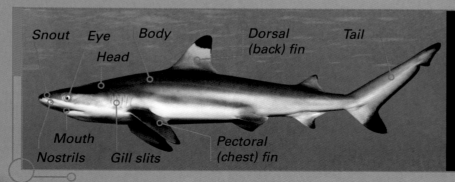

Snout   Eye   Body   Dorsal   Tail
              Head   (back) fin

Mouth
Nostrils   Gill slits   Pectoral
                          (chest) fin

SHARK PARTS
Sharks come in a huge range of shapes and sizes, but they all have the same basic body parts. You can see them on this picture of a blacktip reef shark, a typical-looking shark.

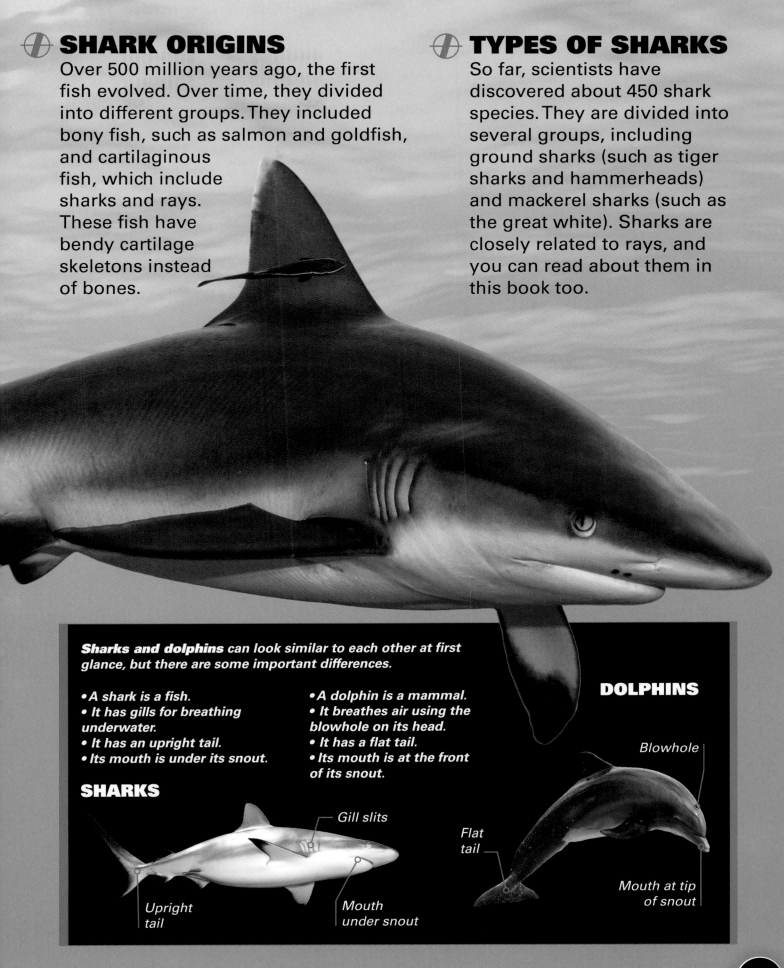

SHARK ORIGINS

Over 500 million years ago, the first fish evolved. Over time, they divided into different groups. They included bony fish, such as salmon and goldfish, and cartilaginous fish, which include sharks and rays. These fish have bendy cartilage skeletons instead of bones.

TYPES OF SHARKS

So far, scientists have discovered about 450 shark species. They are divided into several groups, including ground sharks (such as tiger sharks and hammerheads) and mackerel sharks (such as the great white). Sharks are closely related to rays, and you can read about them in this book too.

Sharks and dolphins can look similar to each other at first glance, but there are some important differences.

- *A shark is a fish.*
- *It has gills for breathing underwater.*
- *It has an upright tail.*
- *Its mouth is under its snout.*

- *A dolphin is a mammal.*
- *It breathes air using the blowhole on its head.*
- *It has a flat tail.*
- *Its mouth is at the front of its snout.*

DOLPHINS

Blowhole

SHARKS

Gill slits

Flat tail

Upright tail

Mouth under snout

Mouth at tip of snout

GREAT WHITE SHARK

The great white is the most famous shark of all, thanks to its huge size, its excellent hunting skills, and its appearance in horror films about shark attacks. However, great whites are actually quite shy, and it's hard for scientists to find out much about them.

BIG FISH

The great white shark really is BIG—it can grow up to 23 feet (7 m) long, and possibly even up to 26 feet (8 m). That means a large great white would only barely fit inside a typical classroom! There are bigger sharks, such as the whale shark and basking shark, but they are filter feeders. They move along slowly, sifting plankton out of the water rather than chasing large prey. So the great white is the world's biggest fast, fierce hunting shark.

Where's the white?
Great white sharks aren't white all over. They are gray on top and cream or white underneath.

FACT FILE

TYPE
Great white shark (Carcharodon carcharias)

FOUND
Cool and medium-warm ocean waters around the world, especially near coasts

DIET
Fish (including other sharks), dolphins, small whales, seals, turtles, seabirds and many other sea creatures

0 | 23 feet (7 m)

SIZE • 16–23 FEET (5–7 M)

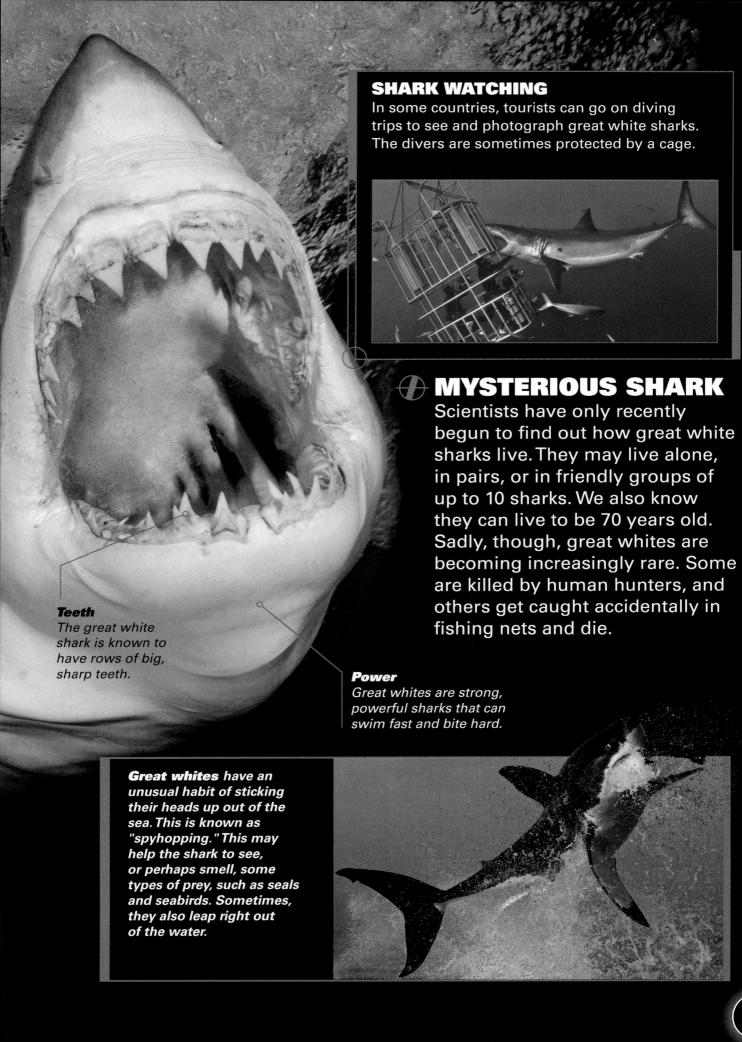

SHARK WATCHING

In some countries, tourists can go on diving trips to see and photograph great white sharks. The divers are sometimes protected by a cage.

⊕ MYSTERIOUS SHARK

Scientists have only recently begun to find out how great white sharks live. They may live alone, in pairs, or in friendly groups of up to 10 sharks. We also know they can live to be 70 years old. Sadly, though, great whites are becoming increasingly rare. Some are killed by human hunters, and others get caught accidentally in fishing nets and die.

Teeth
The great white shark is known to have rows of big, sharp teeth.

Power
Great whites are strong, powerful sharks that can swim fast and bite hard.

Great whites have an unusual habit of sticking their heads up out of the sea. This is known as "spyhopping." This may help the shark to see, or perhaps smell, some types of prey, such as seals and seabirds. Sometimes, they also leap right out of the water.

GREAT HAMMERHEAD SHARK

Fin
The great hammerhead has a very long, pointed dorsal fin.

The bizarre-looking great hammerhead is a fast, fierce, and intelligent shark, and the largest of the hammerhead family. All hammerheads have flat, wide heads that make them look a bit like hammers.

FACT FILE

TYPE
Great hammerhead shark (Sphyrna mokarran)

FOUND
In warm, tropical seas around the world

DIET
Squid, crabs, lobsters and fish, especially rays

0   20 feet (6 m)

SIZE • 10–20 FEET (3–6 M)

HUNTING ALONE

While some types of hammerhead like to swim in groups, the great hammerhead is a solitary predator. It shows no fear of humans and often swims close to divers. However, great hammerheads rarely attack humans, preferring to search for rays, their favorite food.

HAMMERHEAD SENSES

Scientists think the hammerhead's hammer helps the shark to find prey. The eyes and nostrils are far apart, giving it a wide range of vision and helping it to sense which direction a smell is coming from. The hammer also has more electrical sense organs than other sharks, which are used to detect tiny electric signals coming from the bodies of their prey.

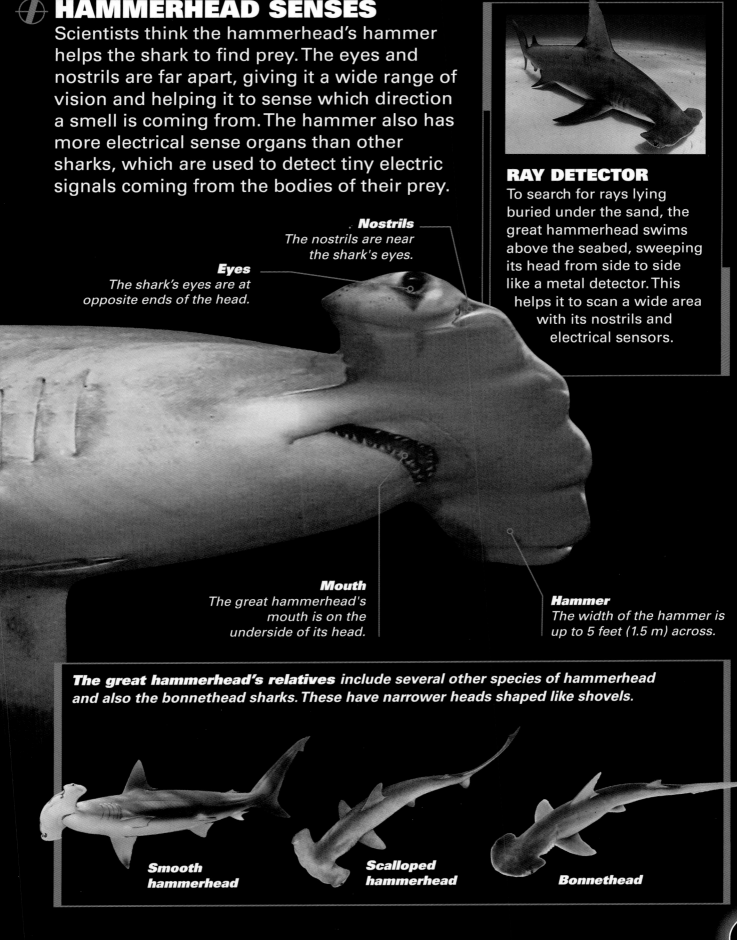

RAY DETECTOR

To search for rays lying buried under the sand, the great hammerhead swims above the seabed, sweeping its head from side to side like a metal detector. This helps it to scan a wide area with its nostrils and electrical sensors.

Nostrils
The nostrils are near the shark's eyes.

Eyes
The shark's eyes are at opposite ends of the head.

Mouth
The great hammerhead's mouth is on the underside of its head.

Hammer
The width of the hammer is up to 5 feet (1.5 m) across.

The great hammerhead's relatives **include several other species of hammerhead and also the bonnethead sharks. These have narrower heads shaped like shovels.**

Smooth hammerhead

Scalloped hammerhead

Bonnethead

BULL SHARK

The bull shark gets its name because, like a bull, it is strong and tough, and can be bad-tempered and aggressive. It is also one of the few sharks that you might find in a river or lake, far away from the sea.

Color
A bull shark is dark gray on top and white underneath.

Eyes
Bull sharks have small eyes and don't rely on eyesight as much as their other senses.

FACT FILE

TYPE
Bull shark (Carcharhinus leucas)

FOUND
Warm and tropical seas near the coast, and some rivers and lakes

DIET
Fish (including other sharks), turtles, seabirds, rays, squid, and even river mammals, such as young hippos, or land mammals, such as dogs and antelopes

0   11½ feet (3.5 m)

SIZE • 6½–11½ FEET (2–3.5 M)

RIVER SHARK

Most sharks live in the sea, and bull sharks do too, but they also have an unusual ability to survive in fresh (non-salty) water. They may swim a long way up rivers into shallow, muddy or shadowy water, where they prefer to hunt. Some even visit large inland lakes, such as Lake Nicaragua in Central America.

SNACKS ON THE SHORE
Bull sharks will hunt any animal they can, if it looks good enough to eat. They sometimes prowl the edges of rivers and grab animals that come into the water to drink or play.

A young hippo could be at risk of a bull shark attack.

GRUMPY SHARKS

Bull sharks have a reputation for being bad-tempered and grumpy, and more likely to bite than many other sharks. This may be because they are often found in shallow water, where they are likely to encounter people swimming, fishing, or bathing. If the shark feels threatened by a human, it may "bump" them with its snout, then come back to bite them.

Scientists have found that bull sharks swim between Lake Nicaragua and the Caribbean Sea along the San Juan River, which is almost 125 miles (200 km) long. The river contains fast-flowing rapids, but the sharks can jump and wriggle their way upstream, in the same way that salmon do.

Lake Nicaragua

Caribbean Sea

San Juan River

Body
Bull sharks have thick, muscular bodies, making them heavy and powerful, although they are not as big as some sharks.

SHARK TEETH

We tend to think of sharks as fierce, scary creatures, partly thanks to their rows of sharp, vicious-looking teeth. All sharks are predators—hunters that feed on other animals—and many of them rely on their teeth to grab and tear up their food.

RAZOR-SHARP

Many sharks' teeth are extremely sharp. Depending on the species, they may be used to cut through raw fish or meat, blubber, bone, the thick, furry skin of a seal, or even a turtle's shell. They often have serrated (jagged) edges, like a bread knife, which makes them even better at cutting.

Tiger shark tooth

NEW TEETH

Many sharks, such as the sand tiger, have rows and rows of teeth. Only the front few rows are used for biting. As these teeth wear away or get broken off, the rows behind move forward to take their place. Some sharks can go through 30,000 teeth in their lifetime.

Because sharks' teeth often fall out, they litter the seabed. Many fossilized sharks' teeth have been found too. The biggest teeth come from a prehistoric shark known as Megalodon. It was similar to a great white shark, but MUCH bigger!

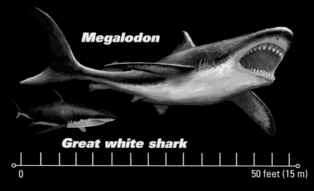

Megalodon

Great white shark

0   50 feet (15 m)

Great white shark tooth

Fossilized Megalodon tooth up to 7 inches (18 cm) long

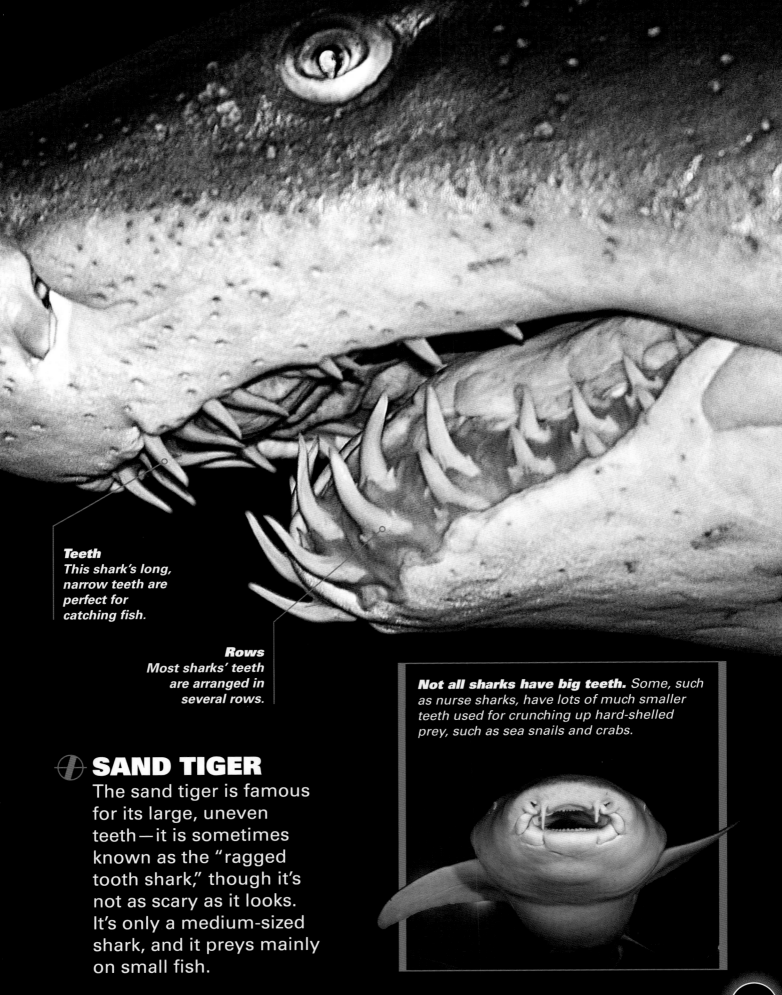

Teeth
This shark's long, narrow teeth are perfect for catching fish.

Rows
Most sharks' teeth are arranged in several rows.

Not all sharks have big teeth. *Some, such as nurse sharks, have lots of much smaller teeth used for crunching up hard-shelled prey, such as sea snails and crabs.*

SAND TIGER

The sand tiger is famous for its large, uneven teeth—it is sometimes known as the "ragged tooth shark," though it's not as scary as it looks. It's only a medium-sized shark, and it preys mainly on small fish.

MAKO SHARKS

FACT FILE

TYPE
Shortfin mako shark
(*Isurus oxyrinchus*)
Longfin mako shark
(*Isurus paucus*)

FOUND
Warm seas around the
world, especially in
the open ocean

DIET
Fish (especially tuna and
swordfish), squid, turtles,
seabirds and porpoises

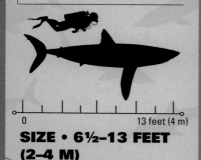

0   13 feet (4 m)

**SIZE • 6½–13 FEET
(2–4 M)**

While some sharks prefer to stay close to the coast, others, such as mako sharks, are "pelagic," meaning they live in the wide open ocean. There they can zoom around at high speed, chasing fast-swimming prey, such as swordfish and tuna.

OCEAN HUNTERS

There are two species of mako shark, the longfin and the shortfin. They swim long distances across the ocean to find and chase other fish. A mako closes in on its prey from behind or below, then grabs it with its sharp teeth, tearing chunks out of it. The injured fish can't swim far, and the mako returns to eat the rest of it.

LONGFIN OR SHORTFIN?

The two makos look similar, but there are some differences. The most obvious is the longfin's extra-large pectoral fins. Longfins also have longer, narrower bodies than shortfins.

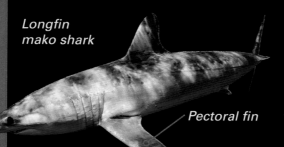

*Longfin
mako shark*

*Shortfin
mako shark*

Pectoral fin

Teeth
A mako's long, sharp, pointed teeth help it to grip slippery fish. You can see the teeth even when the mako's mouth is shut.

FASTEST SHARK

The shortfin mako is the fastest shark in the world. It has been recorded swimming at more than 31 miles per hour (50 kph) and is thought to be able to go even faster. Shortfin makos need speed in order to chase fish such as tuna, which are also fast swimmers. Longfins aren't quite as fast, and prefer slightly slower prey, such as squid.

Shortfin mako
This is a shortfin mako, the more common type of mako shark.

Makos, especially shortfins, are amazing jumpers. They can leap high out of the ocean. They often do this if a fisherman is trying to catch them. A shortfin mako can jump as high as 30 feet (9 m) clear of the surface! To do this, it has to build up a lot of speed underwater, before powering itself up and out into the air.

Streamlined
The mako's pointed, streamlined body shape helps it to move fast through the water.

Eyes
Makos have huge eyes, which help them to spot their prey in murky water.

BLUE SHARK

A great white shark may not be totally white, but a blue shark really is blue! It's a deep, rich, indigo blue on top and paler blue on the sides, fading to a white belly. At about 10 feet (3 m) long, this isn't a huge shark, but it has a very long, narrow shape and can swim fast.

Color
Blue sharks vary from dark to light blue on top, with a paler underside.

Shape
It has a long, slender, streamlined body for swimming fast and far.

Fins
Long pectoral fins help the shark to make fast, accurate movements.

FACT FILE

TYPE
Blue shark (Prionace glauca)

FOUND
Coast and open oceans all around the world, except near the chilly poles

DIET
Fish, squid, octopuses, crabs and lobsters

0   13 feet (4 m)

SIZE • 5–13 FEET (1.5–4 M)

LONG-DISTANCE TRAVELER

Blue sharks don't always swim fast—they often wander around slowly in search of slow-moving prey, such as lobsters—but they do swim far. In a year, a blue shark can travel thousands of miles as it migrates to and fro across the ocean, following currents to find a mate, food and water at a temperature it likes.

DARK AND LIGHT

Why are so many sharks darker on top and paler underneath? It's because this coloration, called "countershading," provides camouflage. As light from above falls on the shark, it leaves the underside in shadow. The countershading helps to cancel out this effect, making the shark harder to see.

Viewed from above, the shark's dark back blends in with the darker depths.

Viewed from below, the shark's paler underside blends with the bright sea surface.

THEY'RE EVERYWHERE!

If you were sailing across the sea and spotted a shark near your ship, the chances are it would be a blue shark. One of the most common of all shark species, it lives in almost all the world's oceans, apart from the coldest waters around the poles. However, each year millions of blue sharks are caught by fishermen for food, which means they could soon start to become endangered.

Weight
Their slender frame means blue sharks weigh less than most sharks.

***Shark fin soup** is a traditional Chinese dish made using the rubbery cartilage in shark fins. It is estimated that as many as 73 million sharks—especially blue sharks—are caught every year to make it. Fishermen often cut off the fins and then throw the sharks back into the ocean, where they die. Some countries have now banned trading in shark fins, and shark fin soup is becoming less popular.*

THRESHER SHARKS

Tail
Threshers are famous for their extra-long tails, which also give them the nickname "fox sharks."

Take a look at the shark on this page and there's something you just can't help noticing—that amazing tail! In some thresher sharks, the upper part (or "lobe") of the tail is as long as the whole of the rest of the shark.

TAKE THAT!

Thresher sharks use their tails not only for swimming, but also for hunting. When a shark finds a shoal of fish, it thrashes its long tail right into the shoal, killing or stunning as many fish as possible before gobbling them up. Two threshers sometimes work together to trap a larger shoal.

A thresher shark stuns its prey with its long tail.

Scientists have identified three species of thresher shark. *(Some think there may also be a fourth, but this isn't known for sure yet.) The three well-known threshers are:*

1) The pelagic thresher
At 10 feet (3 m) long, this is the smallest thresher shark.

2) The bigeye thresher
This 13-foot-long (4 m) shark is named for its very large eyes.

WARM-BODIED SHARKS

Most sharks and other fish are cold-blooded. This means that they stay the same temperature as the water they are in. But a few sharks, including great whites, mako sharks, and common and bigeye threshers, have an unusual ability. They can keep some parts of their bodies extra-warm. This allows their muscles to work better, and to help them move fast.

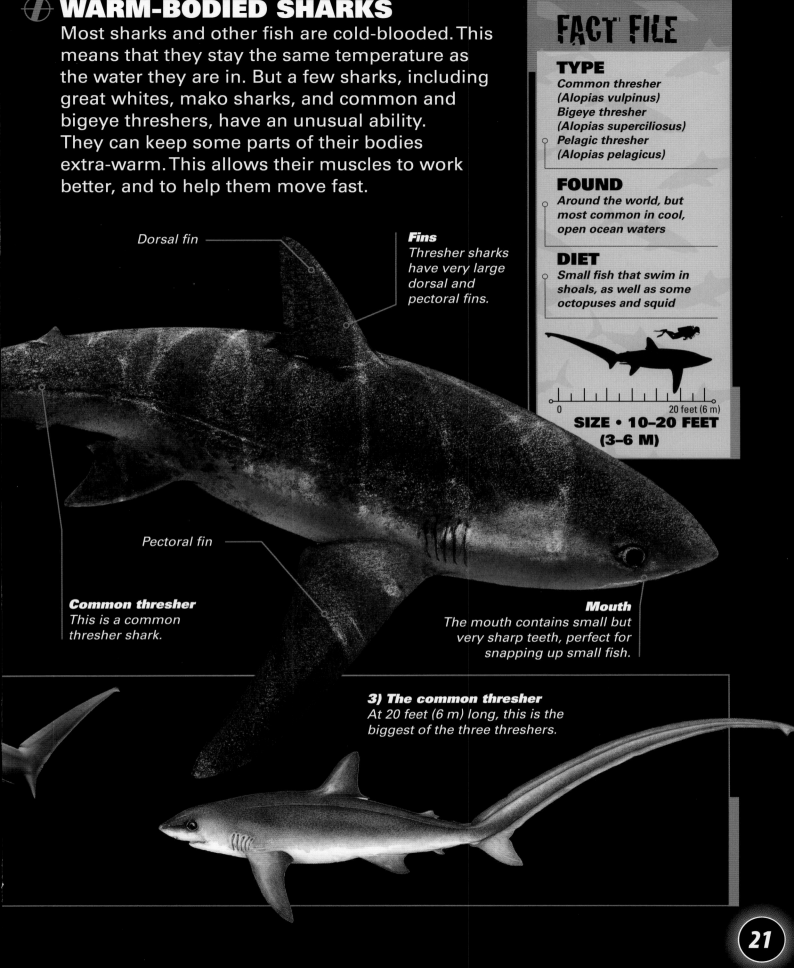

Dorsal fin

Fins
Thresher sharks have very large dorsal and pectoral fins.

Pectoral fin

Common thresher
This is a common thresher shark.

Mouth
The mouth contains small but very sharp teeth, perfect for snapping up small fish.

3) The common thresher
At 20 feet (6 m) long, this is the biggest of the three threshers.

SHARK SKELETONS

Did you know that sharks have no bones? They do have skeletons, but instead of bone, their skeletons are made of cartilage—a flexible, rubbery, lightweight material. This is partly why many sharks are such fast, flexible swimmers.

Body parts
A shark's skeleton includes the skull, jaws, gills, backbone, fins, and tail...

Missing bits
...but unlike the skeleton of a bony fish, it has no ribs.

SHARK JAWS
In bony fish (and in humans), only the lower jaw can move. The upper jaw is part of the skull. Sharks are different! Both their upper and lower jaws are separate from the skull. This means a shark can thrust both its jaws forward, away from its head, to help it grab its prey.

BONY OR BENDY?
There are two main types of fish. Most fish, such as salmon, belong to the bony fish family. Their skeletons are made of bone, just like human skeletons. But sharks, along with their cousins the rays and skates, belong to another family, called cartilaginous fish. They all have skeletons made of cartilage.

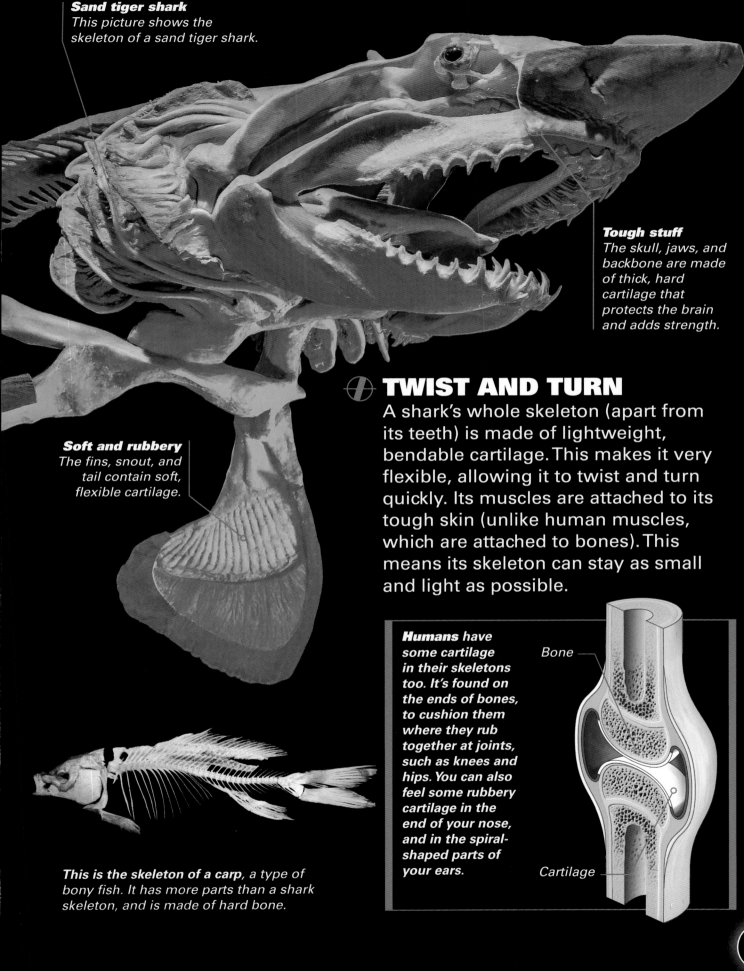

Sand tiger shark
This picture shows the skeleton of a sand tiger shark.

Tough stuff
The skull, jaws, and backbone are made of thick, hard cartilage that protects the brain and adds strength.

Soft and rubbery
The fins, snout, and tail contain soft, flexible cartilage.

TWIST AND TURN

A shark's whole skeleton (apart from its teeth) is made of lightweight, bendable cartilage. This makes it very flexible, allowing it to twist and turn quickly. Its muscles are attached to its tough skin (unlike human muscles, which are attached to bones). This means its skeleton can stay as small and light as possible.

Humans have some cartilage in their skeletons too. It's found on the ends of bones, to cushion them where they rub together at joints, such as knees and hips. You can also feel some rubbery cartilage in the end of your nose, and in the spiral-shaped parts of your ears.

Bone

Cartilage

This is the skeleton of a carp, a type of bony fish. It has more parts than a shark skeleton, and is made of hard bone.

SHARK SKIN

When you see most types of fish, you notice their smooth, shiny scales. But sharks are different. Their scales are more like sharp, tooth-shaped spikes, and are called dermal denticles.

 ## TEETH OF THE SKIN

The name "dermal" means "of the skin," while "denticles" means "little teeth." Dermal denticles grow like teeth, but are anchored into the skin instead of the jaws. They are often tiny— less than half a millimeter long on a spiny dogfish or a mako shark—and tightly packed together. But some sharks, such as the bramble shark, have much bigger, more spread-out denticles that are more like prickly thorns.

SHARK LEATHER

For centuries people have used shark skin as a type of leather, called shagreen. It's used to make items such as shoes, bags, and book covers. Inuit people used the skin of Greenland sharks (page 42) to make tough leather boots. Because the skin is rough, it gives a good grip, so it can also be found on the handles of old weapons, such as swords and bows.

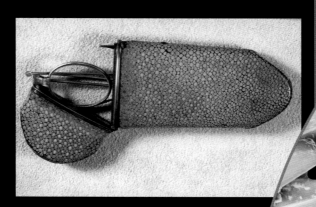

This late 18th-century spectacles case is covered in shagreen.

Flexible
Each denticle is separately rooted into the shark's rubbery skin, so it can still bend and flex.

WHAT ARE THEY FOR?

A shark's dermal denticles give its skin a tough, armor-like covering, making it harder for a predator to bite through. They also help the shark to swim. If you were to stroke a shark from its head toward its tail, its skin would feel very smooth, but in the other direction it would feel rough and resistant. The denticles help water to flow smoothly past the shark, reducing drag and saving energy. Lastly, the rough surface is harder for germs to stick to, helping the shark to stay healthy.

SHARK TECHNOLOGY

Now that scientists have found out how denticles help sharks, they are working on ways to copy them. Adding denticles to swimming costumes or diving gear, for example, could help swimmers to save energy. Scientists have also developed antibacterial surfaces based on shark skin to help stop germs from spreading in hospitals. A material such as this can be used on frequently touched surfaces such as toilet handles or medical machinery.

Ridges
Each denticle has ridges on it, which direct the flow of water along the shark's body.

Spiny dogfish
This shark's skin is shown in close-up (left), seen through a microscope.

Points
The sharp tips of the denticles point backward, toward the shark's tail.

TIGER SHARK

With its big, powerful body, wide mouth, big teeth, and eat-anything attitude, the tiger shark is one of the fiercest predators in the sea. It's also a shark that humans often meet, as it likes coral reefs, harbors, estuaries, and shallow coastal water.

This young tiger shark has clear, stripe-like markings on its sides.

Size
This is the fourth-biggest shark in the world. It can grow to more than 23 feet (7 m) long.

Camouflage
Tiger sharks are greenish-blue on top and creamy white underneath, to match their shallow-water habitat.

FACT FILE

TYPE
Tiger shark
(Galeocerdo cuvier)

FOUND
Mainly around coasts in warm and tropical seas

DIET
Fish, jellyfish, octopuses, squid, rays, dolphins, seals, turtles, small whales—and much more!

0   23 feet (7 m)

SIZE • 10–23 FEET (3–7 M)

TIGER OF THE SEA
The tiger shark is named "tiger" because it has stripes! These can be hard to see on an adult shark, because they fade as the shark grows, but they are clearly visible on baby and young tiger sharks.

LIVING TRASH CAN

Tiger sharks have an amazing ability to eat almost anything. As well as gobbling up pretty much any sea creature they come across (alive or dead), they have been known to eat land animals that enter the water, including dogs, goats, and even horses! But it doesn't stop there. Scientists have discovered all kinds of non-food items in tiger sharks' stomachs, including oil cans, baseballs, car tires, beer bottles, and an old raincoat.

SEEING IN THE DARK

Like real tigers, tiger sharks have good eyesight and often hunt at night. A tiger shark can quickly adjust its vision to low light levels, helping it to home in on prey hiding among coral reefs or in murky sea caves. When hunting, the shark will prowl around slowly and quietly, then pounce on its prey with a sudden burst of speed.

Mouth
Tiger sharks have big mouths for grabbing large prey.

Large sharks usually have very few predators—they are at the top of the food chain. But in 2014, a pod or group of orcas (killer whales) was filmed working together to surround and attack an unlucky tiger shark. Tiger sharks also sometimes do the same to a whale!

LEMON SHARK

The lemon shark gets its name because, unusually for a shark, it has a yellowish tinge, or sometimes a brownish mustard color. This gives it camouflage against sandy, sunny seabeds in shallow water, where it likes to live.

Young sharks can become prey for other types of sharks, but mangrove roots act as a protective cage.

LIVING TOGETHER

Some sharks live and hunt alone, but lemon sharks are often found in groups. Very young lemon sharks like to live among the roots of coastal mangrove trees, which stand on their roots in shallow seawater. This helps them to hide from danger. Older sharks are often found in shallow lagoons.

Eyes
These sharks have sharp eyesight, and are good at seeing fine detail and different colors.

Scientists have found that lemon sharks can live happily and survive well in captivity. This is unusual. Most large sharks die after just a few days in an aquarium. You can sometimes see a lemon shark in a public aquarium, and they are also kept in special shark laboratories, where scientists study the way they behave. We know more about the lives of lemon sharks than any other shark species.

BRAINY SHARKS

Scientists who study lemon sharks have found that the sharks have quite big brains (for a shark!), and are good at learning. This is probably a result of living in groups. Animals that share a home and do things together are often good at learning skills, such as hunting methods, from each other.

WE DON'T BITE!

Lemon sharks have a gentle, friendly nature, probably also a result of living in groups. They have never been known to eat a human, and have only attacked people who deliberately annoyed them.

Cleaners
Fish called remoras eat parasites on the shark's skin and help keep it clean.

FACT FILE

TYPE
Lemon shark (Negaprion brevirostris)

FOUND
Shallow waters along coasts and around islands and reefs in the Atlantic Ocean and Pacific Ocean

DIET
Mainly bony fish, along with some rays, crabs and seabirds

0   10 feet (3 m)

SIZE • 6½–10 FEET (2–3 M)

Shallow swimmer
Lemon sharks are often found in shallow, sunlit water.

Body
The lemon shark's wide, flattish body and snout are perfect for prowling the seabed.

GOBLIN SHARK

FACT FILE

TYPE
Goblin shark
(Mitsukurina owstoni)

FOUND
Lives in water over
330 feet (100 m) deep,
off coasts and islands

DIET
Fish, squid, rays and crabs

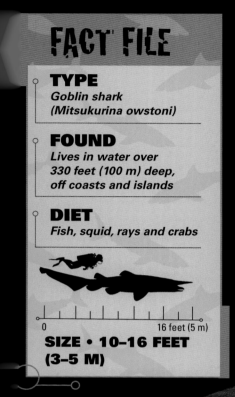

0   16 feet (5 m)

**SIZE • 10–16 FEET
(3–5 M)**

It's rare, pink, flabby, and extremely strange-looking. Meet the goblin shark! This deep-water species, rarely seen by humans, is one of the world's weirdest and least understood sharks.

Tail
The tail is long
and slender.

Pink
It looks pinkish because
you can see its blood
vessels through its skin.

LIVING FOSSIL

When goblin sharks were first discovered, scientists realized they were very unusual and not closely related to any other shark. But then they noticed that goblin sharks do resemble some ancient shark fossils, such as *Scapanorhynchus*, which lived about 100 million years ago. The goblin shark's relatives probably died out long ago, and it is the only shark of its type left. Animals such as this are sometimes known as "living fossils."

The extinct shark Scapanorhynchus
looked similar to a goblin shark.

SHARK OF THE DEEP

The goblin shark rarely comes close to the surface, preferring to stay near the deep seabed as much as 3,300 feet (1,000 m) below the surface. There, it feeds on smaller fish and squid, and crustaceans such as crabs and shrimp. People usually only encounter goblin sharks when the sharks are accidentally caught in deep-sea fishing nets and get hauled to the surface.

Flabby
The goblin shark is soft and flabby, which probably means it's a slow mover.

Snout
The unusual snout is wide, pointed, and flat, like a sword blade.

Teeth
This shark has distinctive, needle-like teeth.

CURIOUS SHARK

Though goblin sharks don't have any history of attacking people, they seem fascinated with undersea cables, and often try to nibble them. Their teeth are often found stuck into cable coverings. They have also been known to chew on divers' wetsuits

All sharks can thrust their jaws forward, but goblin sharks do it more than most! The shark's jaws can shoot right out under its long snout to grab prey. Combined with its staring, beady eyes, snaggly teeth, and pink skin, this makes the goblin shark look fascinatingly strange and monstrous.

This is a dead goblin shark from a fisherman's net.

SHARK SENSES

Sharks are meat-eaters and use their senses to track down their prey. Like us, they have senses of sight, smell, taste, touch and hearing. They also have a sixth sense that can detect electricity (see pages 34–35).

DO SHARKS HAVE EARS?

Sharks do have ears, but you can barely see them! Two tiny holes on the outside lead to the ears, which are inside the shark's head. Sharks are especially good at hearing low, rumbling noises, which travel well through water. This may be how they find some types of prey.

EYES
Sharks' eyes are on the sides of their heads, giving them a wide range of vision.

EARS
Sharks have ears that look like two tiny holes on the top of the shark's head.

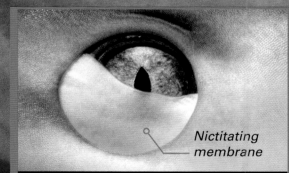

Nictitating membrane

A shark's eyes can open up to let in more light, for example at night or in murky water. When attacking, some sharks protect their eyes from danger by rolling them back into their heads. Others cover them with a kind of eyelid called a "nictitating membrane."

TASTE

Sharks do seem to have taste buds, but we don't know much about their sense of taste. They probably use it, along with their sense of smell, to detect chemicals in the water.

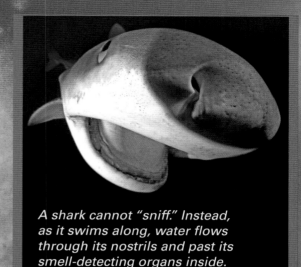

A shark cannot "sniff." Instead, as it swims along, water flows through its nostrils and past its smell-detecting organs inside.

SMELL

Sharks are famous for their excellent sense of smell, which can detect a tiny amount of blood floating in seawater. They can also sniff out a seal colony, a rotting whale, or another shark to mate with. Scientists think that when a shark smells something it wants, it swims into the current, which takes it to where the smell comes from.

Nares
Sharks have two nostrils called "nares" on their snouts.

A WORLD OF TOUCH

Just like us, sharks can feel when something touches them. They often "bump" prey, enemies, or strange objects with their snouts to feel what they are. But they also have an extra touch sense. Sensitive lateral lines along the sides of their bodies detect pressure changes in the water. This means sharks can actually feel the movements of other animals swimming nearby.

Lateral line

SIXTH SENSE

Did you know that your body is buzzing with electricity right now? Animals (including humans) use tiny electrical signals to make their brains, hearts, and muscles work, and to send messages around their bodies. Sharks can detect this, using their sixth sense of "electroreception."

A lemon shark uses electroreception to scan the seabed for food.

Electricity-detecting organs
The little dark dots all over this great white shark's snout, face, and head are its electricity-detecting organs, called the ampullae of Lorenzini.

⊕ ELECTRIC FIELDS

When fish and other creatures move, the electrical activity in their bodies creates an electric field, or area, in the water around them. If a shark is close enough—within about 6 inches (15 cm)—it can sense this. Electroreception is especially useful for hunting in the dark, or for finding prey such as flatfish that lie hidden under sand on the seabed.

⊕ HOW MANY?

A typical shark has over 1,000 electricity-sensing ampullae, and some sharks, such as hammerheads (which have very wide snouts) can have as many as 3,000. They are arranged close to the shark's mouth, as the shark uses them most when it is about to snap up its prey.

DO HUMANS HAVE IT?

Humans don't have an electric sense in the way that sharks do. However, some people say they are sensitive to strong electric fields. They can tell when they are close to an overhead power line, even if they can't see it. In tests, scientists have found that this is true, although people can't sense the tiny amounts of electricity that a shark can.

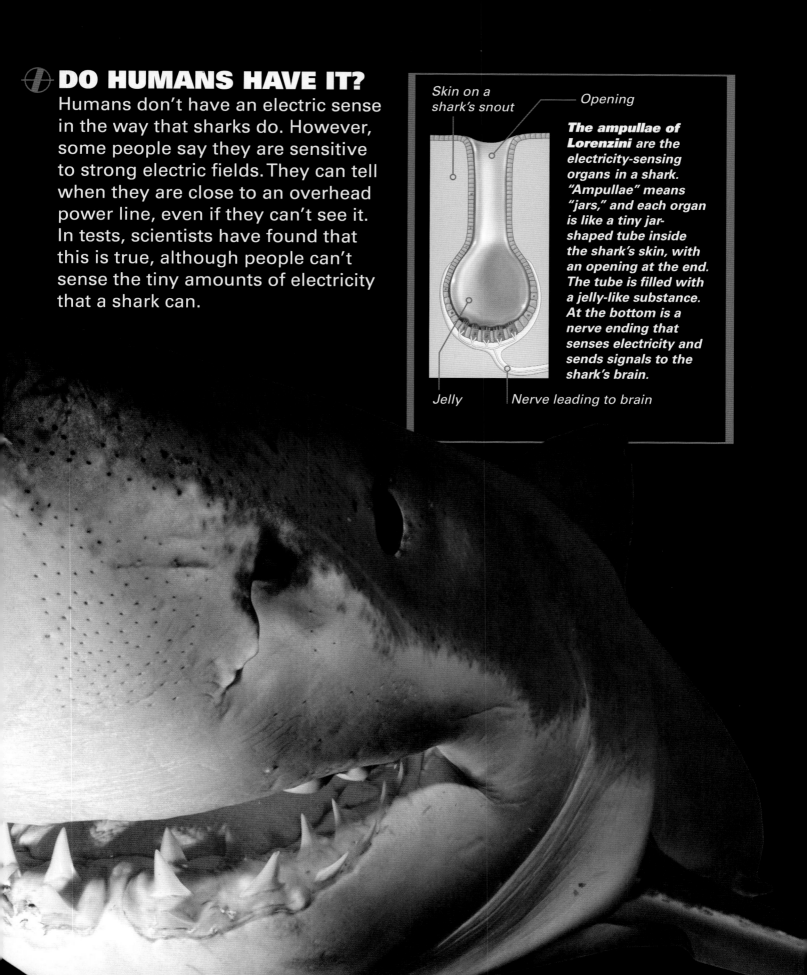

Skin on a shark's snout

Opening

The ampullae of Lorenzini are the electricity-sensing organs in a shark. "Ampullae" means "jars," and each organ is like a tiny jar-shaped tube inside the shark's skin, with an opening at the end. The tube is filled with a jelly-like substance. At the bottom is a nerve ending that senses electricity and sends signals to the shark's brain.

Jelly

Nerve leading to brain

WOBBEGONG SHARKS

If you were snorkeling on a coral reef in Australia or Indonesia, there's a good chance that you might accidentally stand on a wobbegong! These amazing sharks have such excellent camouflage that they can become almost invisible.

CARPET SHARKS

Wobbegongs belong to a family of sharks known as carpet sharks. This group includes a wide range of other sharks too, including zebra sharks, nurse sharks, and the enormous whale shark (see page 48). But none of these sharks looks quite as much like an actual carpet as a wobbegong shark!

FACT FILE

TYPE
Wobbegong sharks
(12 species)
(Orectolobus)

FOUND
Warm, shallow waters around coasts and coral reefs in southeast Asia, Australia and Japan

DIET
Fish, octopuses, crabs, lobsters and shrimp

0   10 feet (3 m)

SIZE • 1½–10 FEET (0.5–3 M)

Eyes
Even the shark's eyes look brownish and speckled.

Barbels
Fleshy barbels near the nostrils are used to taste and feel.

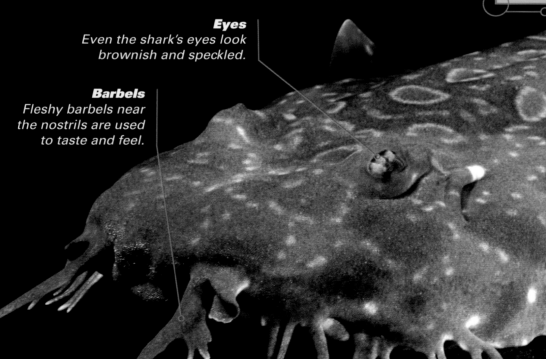

SHARKS IN HIDING

Most wobbegongs have wide, flattened bodies and heads, and they like to lie flat on the seabed. As well as being flat, wobbegongs are covered in speckled and patterned, carpet-like markings. These camouflage them against sand, rocks, seaweeds, and corals. All 12 species of wobbegongs live in shallow seas, mainly around southeast Asia and Australia. They often catch prey by lying still and blending in with their surroundings, then suddenly pouncing on any fish, shrimp, or octopus that swims close enough.

BIG AND SMALL

Wobbegongs come in a range of sizes. The smallest, the network wobbegong, only grows to about 20 inches (50 cm) long, but others can be much bigger. Spotted wobbegongs sometimes reach 10 feet (3 m) long—similar in size to a real carpet!

The rarely seen northern wobbegong is no bigger than a small dog.

Spots
Wobbegongs have speckles and spots of brown, orange, yellow, or gray.

Fins
The wobbegong's fins, like its body, are shaped for lying flat on the seabed.

Spotted wobbegong
This spotted wobbegong is one of the largest species of wobbegong shark.

Most wobbegongs *have frilly, finger-like parts sticking out around their mouths and sometimes their bodies. Some of these just provide extra camouflage among the seaweed, but others, called barbels, can feel and taste their surroundings, helping the wobbegong to find its prey. The tasseled wobbegong (shown here) has the most impressive barbels.*

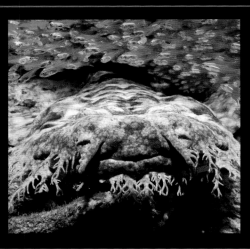

LANTERNSHARKS

Hold your hands together, palms upward. Could you hold a shark in them? Yes! There are some sharks that could fit there, mainly belonging to the lanternshark family. The smallest sharks of all are about the size of a banana—they can be quite hard to spot in the vast ocean.

DEEP AND DARK

This is the velvet belly lanternshark, which can be found more than 6,500 feet (2,000 m) down in the deep sea. Not much sunlight reaches this depth, so the water is very dark and murky, even during the day. The lanternshark has large eyes to help it spot both prey and predators (hunting animals that want to eat it).

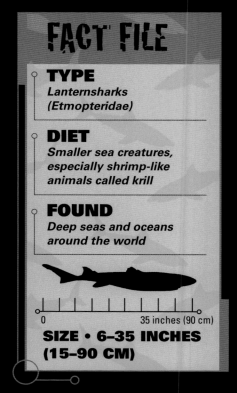

FACT FILE

TYPE
Lanternsharks
(Etmopteridae)

DIET
Smaller sea creatures, especially shrimp-like animals called krill

FOUND
Deep seas and oceans around the world

0   35 inches (90 cm)

SIZE • 6–35 INCHES (15–90 CM)

Head
The head has a snake-like, flattened shape.

Eyes
Its large, rectangle-shaped eyes help the lanternshark to see in dark water.

Size
This isn't the smallest shark of all, but it's still quite tiny. This picture is about life size!

Snout and teeth
Under its snout the shark has lots of tiny but sharp teeth, perfect for grabbing krill.

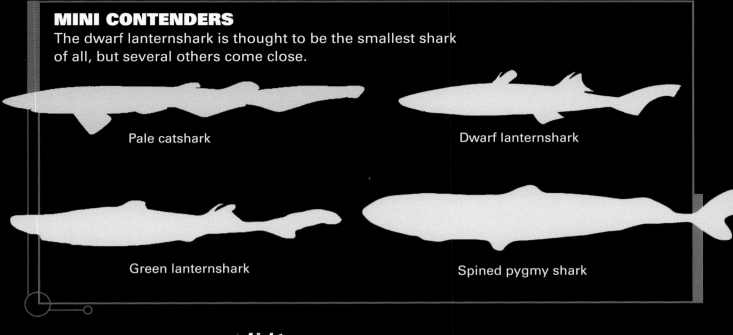

MINI CONTENDERS

The dwarf lanternshark is thought to be the smallest shark of all, but several others come close.

Pale catshark

Dwarf lanternshark

Green lanternshark

Spined pygmy shark

Lights
The shark's skin is mostly brownish black, but it has rows of glowing dots, called photophores, that light up.

LIGHTING UP

Many deep-sea fish, including several sharks, are bioluminescent, meaning they can light up. The velvet belly lanternshark is one of a whole family of lanternsharks that can all glow with their own light. The lights are on the shark's belly and sides, which may give it camouflage when seen from below against the lighter sea surface. The glow is also thought to attract prey animals, which the shark then snaps up.

The spiny dogfish grows to about 4 feet (1.2 m) long.

Dogfish sharks are the group of sharks that lanternsharks belong to. There are about 120 species, making up about a quarter of all sharks, and they are found all over the world. While dwarf lanternsharks are rare, some dogfish, such as the spiny dogfish, are very common.

COOKIECUTTER SHARK

Sharks are meat-eaters, so they don't eat cookies...do they? The cookiecutter shark gets its name because it feeds by biting perfectly round, cookie-sized chunks out of larger animals, using its strangely shaped mouth. Ouch!

COOKIE TIME!

Cookiecutter sharks do sometimes eat whole prey, such as small squid or fish. But they've also found another way to feed. Patterns and glowing lights on a cookiecuttter's body attract large predators. Before the predators have a chance to attack, the cookiecutter turns and quickly latches onto the larger animal, using its sucking lips and small upper teeth to cling on. It then spins around in a circle, using its lower teeth to cut a disc of its victim's skin, which it eats up.

A bite from a cookiecutter shark has scarred the smooth skin of this Hawaiian spinner dolphin.

SCARRED FOR LIFE

Great white sharks, whales, tuna, dolphins, and many other animals have been found with the neat, round scars in their skin left by cookiecutter sharks. On the plus side, at least they escape with their lives!

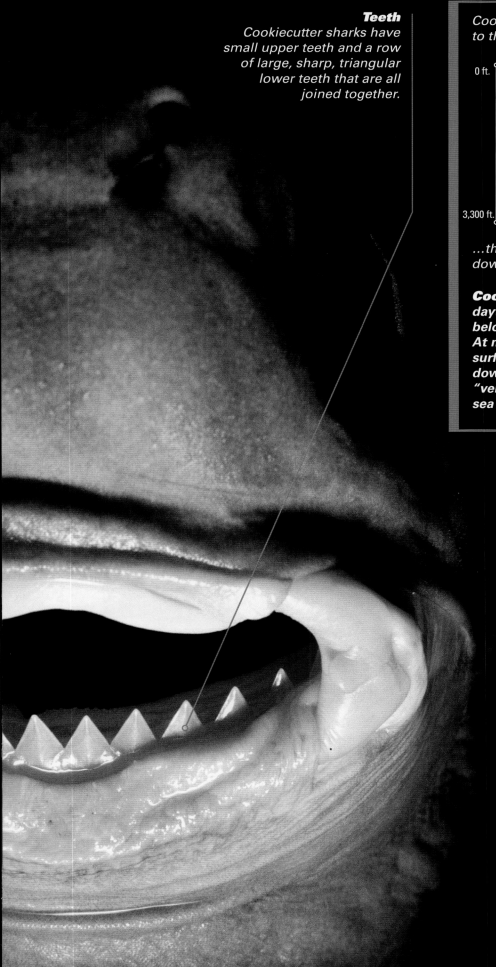

Teeth
Cookiecutter sharks have small upper teeth and a row of large, sharp, triangular lower teeth that are all joined together.

Cookiecutters move up to the surface at dusk...

0 ft.

3,300 ft.

...then back down at dawn.

Cookiecutter sharks *spend the daytime deep down in the ocean, below about 3,300 feet (1,000 m). At night, they swim up toward the surface to feed, and then swim back down before dawn. This is called "vertical migration," and many other sea creatures, such as krill, do it too.*

COOKIE-CUT CABLES

Cookiecutters sometimes bite the plastic coverings of undersea cables and the rubber parts of submarines, and can cause serious damage. They probably do this because plastic and rubber have a similar texture to shark or whale skin. There have also been a few cases of cookiecutters biting humans.

GREENLAND SHARK

Most sharks are found in hot areas close to the Equator, or in medium-warm seas such as the Mediterranean. You might not expect to find a shark under the Arctic ice, but that's home for the giant Greenland shark.

DON'T EAT ME!

Greenland shark flesh contains a chemical called urea, which is also found in urine (pee!). It's poisonous to humans. However, dried, rotted Greenland shark, known as hákarl, is safe to eat, and is a popular delicacy in Iceland.

Hákarl has a strange, jelly-like texture and a strong taste, and many people find it revolting!

Eyes
This huge shark has quite small eyes and poor eyesight.

SHARK OF THE NORTH

The Greenland shark is found further north than any other shark species. It is happiest in water that's close to freezing, and can be spotted around the coasts of Norway, Iceland, Canada, Russia and Greenland. It sometimes lives further south too, but only in very deep water, where the water temperature is much colder than it is at the surface.

SLEEPER SHARKS

Greenland sharks are one of a group of dogfish sharks known as sleeper sharks, because of their slow, lazy-looking movements. A Greenland shark likes to wander along at about 1 mph (1.5 kph), which is slower than most people walk. Instead of chasing its prey, it may sneak up quietly on fish and snap them up, or grab seals that have their heads out of the water. Greenland sharks also sniff out and feed on carrion (dead animals), such as whales, or even reindeer that have fallen into the sea.

Greenland sharks can't see very well, and many of them have strange creatures permanently attached to their eyes! The 2-inch-long (5 cm) parasite is a type of copepod, a crustacean related to crabs and shrimp. It fixes itself to the shark's eyeball and nibbles on it. This damages the shark's eyesight, but the shark can still survive, using its sense of smell to find food.

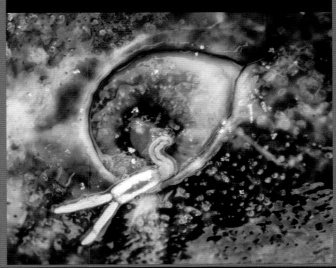

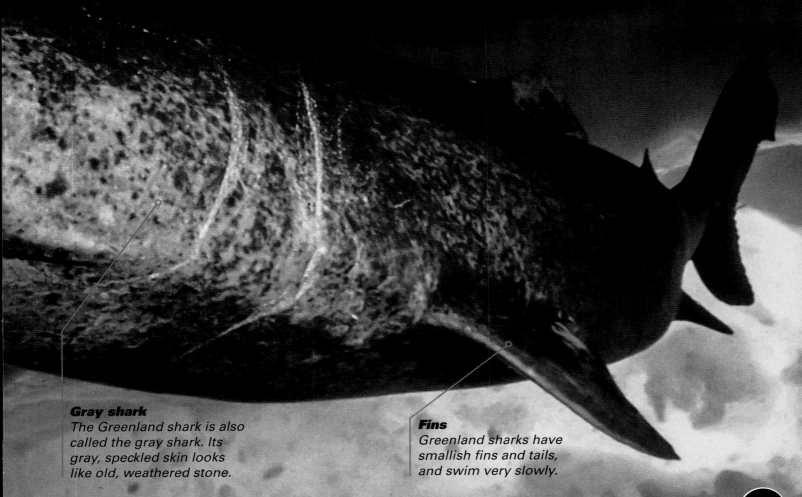

Gray shark
The Greenland shark is also called the gray shark. Its gray, speckled skin looks like old, weathered stone.

Fins
Greenland sharks have smallish fins and tails, and swim very slowly.

SHARK EGGS

Most fish have their babies by laying eggs. But many sharks don't! There are about 450 species of sharks, but fewer then 200 of these are oviparous, meaning they lay eggs. The others give birth to live babies (see pages 46–47).

(see pages 46–47)

MERMAID'S PURSES

After the pups hatch, the empty egg cases are left behind, and often wash up on beaches. They are sometimes called "mermaid's purses."

Swell shark egg

Small-spotted catshark egg

Tendrils
Stringy tendrils help the cases to get caught in crevices or other safe places.

Egg case
The egg is protected by a hard case.

Embryo
The unborn baby shark, or embryo, grows inside the egg case.

⊕ EGGS AND EGG CASES

When sharks do lay eggs, each egg is enclosed inside a protective egg case. These come in a range of shapes and sizes, depending on the species of shark that laid them. They often have dangling strings or tendrils that get caught among seaweed or coral. This helps the eggs to stay safe and not get carried away by the current.

Whose eggs?
Inside are baby dogfish sharks.

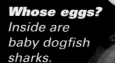

Zebra shark egg

Undulate ray egg

Bamboo shark egg

⊕ GROWING AND HATCHING

Sharks don't take care of or feed their babies—once the mother shark has laid her eggs, she leaves them alone. Inside the egg case, the baby shark feeds on the egg yolk and grows bigger. Eventually it is almost as big as the egg case and can be seen wriggling around inside the case. When it is ready to be born, the baby shark, called a pup, hatches out of the case. From then on, it has to find its own food.

The female horn shark lays two spiral-shaped eggs at a time. Before leaving them, she picks them up and wedges them into a safe place, such as a crack between rocks. Their spiral shape makes it very difficult for a predator to pull them out from their hiding places.

Sharks that give birth to live babies or "pups" are known as viviparous sharks. They include many well-known species, such as great whites, makos, tiger sharks and hammerheads.

EATING EACH OTHER

Sand tiger shark pups are very fierce, even before they are born! A pregnant mother sand tiger starts off with up to 50 pups growing inside her, but the biggest, strongest ones eat the others, until only two are left.

This pregnant sand tiger shark will soon give birth.

Swimming away
A baby shark doesn't stay with its mother. Soon after being born, it swims off to look for food.

GROWING UP

A newborn human, kitten, or bird needs lots of care and has to be fed by its parents. But a newborn shark can swim, hunt, and eat meat right away. However, being very small, shark pups are in danger of being eaten by other sea creatures. To stay safe, some shark pups have more camouflage than their parents. Tiger and zebra shark pups, for example, have stripe markings that they lose as they grow up (see page 26).

HOW MANY BABIES?

Because some pups get eaten before they can become adults, many shark species have lots of babies to make sure that some will survive. A female whale shark can give birth to more than 100 pups in a litter. However, some sharks, such as the great white, only have one or two babies at a time. Shark species that have few babies find it hard to recover and build up their numbers if they become endangered.

Shark placenta
Like human babies, some baby sharks are fed by a placenta via an umbilical cord.

In the open ocean, baby sharks swim away from their mothers and off into the unknown. But lemon sharks have nursery areas, where the babies stay for several years. Although their parents don't look after them, being in a nursery area may help them to learn how to hunt by watching older sharks.

A shark scientist holds a baby lemon shark in a shark nursery in the Bahamas. (Photo taken from underwater.)

WHALE SHARK

You're swimming in a warm tropical sea when you see a cavernous mouth 5 feet (1.5 m) wide looming toward you through the water! You've just met a whale shark, the biggest fish in the world. But don't worry—despite their huge mouths, whale sharks don't eat people.

Friendly
Whale sharks are known for their gentle nature, and are happy to swim alongside human divers.

Mouth
The shark's mouth is so big that when it's wide open, you could fit a piano inside!

The whale shark has a very big, wide head and mouth, but its body narrows and tapers toward its tail. When seen from above, this gives it a distinctive shape a bit like a giant tadpole.

SUPERSIZED SHARK

This shark really is the massive monster of the fish world. The biggest whale shark ever recorded measured more than 39 feet (12 m) long, but many people have reported seeing much bigger ones, some up to 60 or even 65 feet (18 or 20 m) long. That's as long as a train car!

SPOTS AND STRIPES

The whale shark is a member of the carpet shark family, which means it's related to wobbegongs and zebra sharks. It's very unlike them in some ways—it's much bigger, and likes the open ocean rather than seabeds and reefs—but like its cousins, it has beautiful markings.

Each whale shark has its own unique pattern of spots and stripes.

Spotted
The whale shark's markings are unlike any other shark's.

FILTER FEEDER

Whale sharks don't hunt large prey such as seals and tuna. They are filter feeders, which means they feed by filtering small creatures out of the water. The shark swims along slowly, taking big gulps of water that then flow out through its gills. The gills have filter pads on them, a bit like sieves, that let water escape while the food moves toward the shark's throat to be swallowed.

MEGAMOUTH SHARK

In 1976, when the crew of a ship off the coast of Hawaii pulled up their anchor, they were in for a surprise. Entangled in the chain was a big, blubbery, and very large-mouthed shark. It was a brand new species, previously unknown to science, and was named the megamouth.

A NEW DISCOVERY

Fishermen and scientists have encountered most types of shark for centuries. It's very unusual to discover a completely unknown species, especially a large one such as the megamouth. Since it was discovered, fewer than 100 megamouths have ever been spotted. Most of these have been accidentally caught in fishing nets, but a few have been filmed in the wild. There could even be other undiscovered sharks out there, roaming around in the deep ocean.

Tail
The tail has an extra-long upper lobe, like a thresher shark's tail.

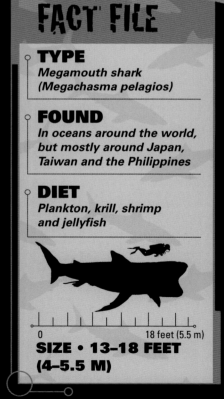

Body
The megamouth's body is thick, heavy, and flabby, and it swims along slowly.

FACT FILE

TYPE
Megamouth shark (Megachasma pelagios)

FOUND
In oceans around the world, but mostly around Japan, Taiwan and the Philippines

DIET
Plankton, krill, shrimp and jellyfish

0   18 feet (5.5 m)

SIZE • 13–18 FEET (4–5.5 M)

1) Whale shark, 39 feet (12 m)

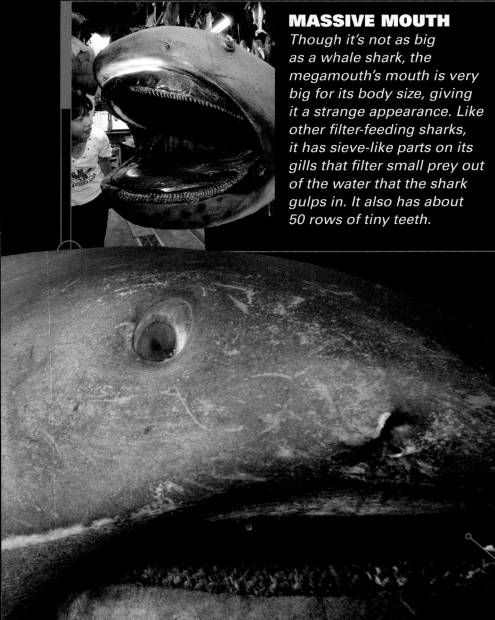

MASSIVE MOUTH

Though it's not as big as a whale shark, the megamouth's mouth is very big for its body size, giving it a strange appearance. Like other filter-feeding sharks, it has sieve-like parts on its gills that filter small prey out of the water that the shark gulps in. It also has about 50 rows of tiny teeth.

TRACKING THE MEGAMOUTH

In 1990, scientists attached a radio tag to a megamouth and tracked its movements over two days. They found that, bumbling along very slowly, it moved close to the surface every night to feed, then swam down to a depth of about 650 feet (200 m) during the day to follow its prey, such as krill.

Head
The head is huge and rounded.

Mouth
The shark's wide mouth wraps right around the front of its snout.

There are only three known sharks that survive by filter feeding. They are all quite different from each other, but they are all pretty big!

2) Basking shark, 26 feet (8 m)

3) Megamouth, 16 feet (5 m)

FRILLED SHARK

If you saw this face looming at you out of the deep, dark water, you might think you'd just seen a sea monster or a strange, swimming dinosaur! The rare and strange-looking frilled shark has existed since the time of the dinosaurs, and is a "living fossil."

The frilled shark has more than 300 teeth, each with three needle-like points on it. The points lean back toward the shark's throat, to help it grip its prey.

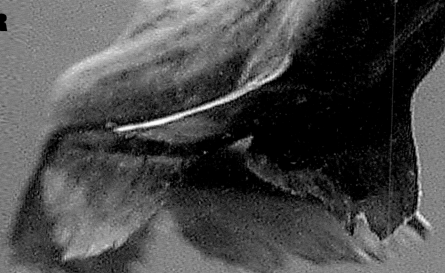

Body
The body is long like an eel's, with the fins set far back.

DEEP-SEA GULPER
We don't know much about frilled sharks, as they live in deep water and are rarely seen. However, by looking inside their stomachs, scientists have discovered that frilled sharks eat fish and squid up to half their own size. They can open their mouths very wide to gulp down large prey.

Frilled sharks seem to swim quite slowly, so scientists aren't sure how they catch fast-moving prey such as large squid. One theory is that the shark can "hover" quietly in the water until prey is nearby, then bend its flexible body back and strike suddenly, like a snake.

SEA SERPENT

Because of its snake-like looks, scientists think sightings of the frilled shark could explain some of the tales about strange sea serpents told by sailors in the past. However, frilled sharks aren't all that big—they only grow to about the same size as a human. So some scientists think there might be a larger, more monstrous species of frilled shark still out there, waiting to be discovered.

Lizard head
The shark's flattened head and snapping jaws give it a lizard-like appearance.

Frills
The shark gets its name from its unusual gills. Some reach right around its neck and look like a frilly collar.

53

REEF SHARKS

If you'd like to meet a real, live shark in the wild, the best place to go is probably a coral reef. Reefs have plenty of fish, octopuses, and other shark food, coral caves to hide in, and sandy shallows to explore—as well as large numbers of reef sharks.

REEF LIFE

A coral reef is a slow-growing structure made by tiny animals called coral polyps. Over time, their shell-like coral skeletons build up to form a reef. Blacktip reef sharks like the shallowest water, where they hunt small fish. Gray and Caribbean reef sharks patrol the deeper water where the reef meets the open ocean. Whitetip reef sharks rest on the seabed or in coral caves by day, and come out at night to hunt.

Not too big
Reef sharks, such as this whitetip, are usually less than 10 feet (3 m) long, and can fit into reef crevices and caves.

FACT FILE

TYPE
*Blacktip reef shark
(Carcharhinus melanopterus)
Whitetip reef shark
(Triaenodon obesus)
Gray reef shark
(Carcharhinus amblyrhynchos)
Caribbean reef shark
(Carcharhinus perezii)*

FOUND
*Warm, shallow waters
around coral reefs*

DIET
*Fish, squid, octopuses, rays,
shrimp, crabs and lobsters*

0   10 feet (3 m)

**SIZE • 3–10 FEET
(1–3 M)**

Remora
Dead skin and parasites on the shark's skin are eaten by remora.

CLEANING STATIONS

Reef sharks will happily gobble up most small reef fish. But sometimes they visit "cleaning stations" on the reef, where fish called cleaner fish nibble parasites from their bodies, or even from inside their mouths. This helps them both; the shark gets cleaned, and the cleaner fish gets a free meal!

A whitetip reef shark opens its mouth wide to let a cleaner fish safely inside.

SOCIAL SHARKS

Many shark species are solitary—they live and hunt alone—but reef sharks usually live in groups. They rest, bask in the sun, and even hunt in packs. Blacktip reef sharks are especially good at this. They will get together to surround a shoal of fish and force them to swim toward the shallowest water close to the shore, where they can be easily snapped up.

In the shallows
Reef sharks patrol the shallow waters around corals in search of food.

Normal position

Threat display

Gray reef sharks are known for their threat display, which warns an enemy that they may attack. They sometimes do it to divers if they get too close. The shark points its pectoral fins down, lifts its snout and curves its body into an "S" shape.

SHARK STORIES

Imagine a shark that can take human shape and come walking onto the land! That's just one of many myths, legends, stories, and traditional beliefs about sharks. They are especially common in the islands of the Pacific, where sharks are often seen.

This Aboriginal rock carving of a shark is in Davidson National Park, Sydney, Australia.

This carving from the Cook Islands shows Avatea, a half-human, half-shark god.

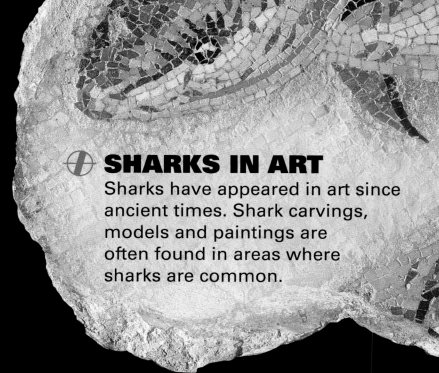

⊕ SHARKS IN ART

Sharks have appeared in art since ancient times. Shark carvings, models and paintings are often found in areas where sharks are common.

SHARK GODS

The islands of Hawaii have not just one but several shark gods as part of their traditional beliefs. The most famous, Kamohoali'i, or the King of Sharks, was said to be able to take the form of any fish, or a human man. Another shark god, Dakuwaqa, comes from the island of Fiji. He was said to have a human body with a shark's head, and protected fishermen from danger.

SHARK BELIEFS

• In Kenya, people say the whale shark got its spots when God threw silver coins down from heaven into the sea and onto the shark's back.

• In Vietnam, the whale shark was traditionally seen as a god and is named "Ca Ong" or "Sir Fish."

• Sailors used to say sharks would follow a ship if someone on board was very ill, hoping they would die and be thrown overboard. In fact, sharks often follow ships in search of food scraps.

• One mistaken belief says that sharks rarely get ill, so eating certain parts of sharks can cure diseases. In fact, sharks can get ill! It's just that we rarely see it happen.

Whale sharks are covered in spots like silver coins.

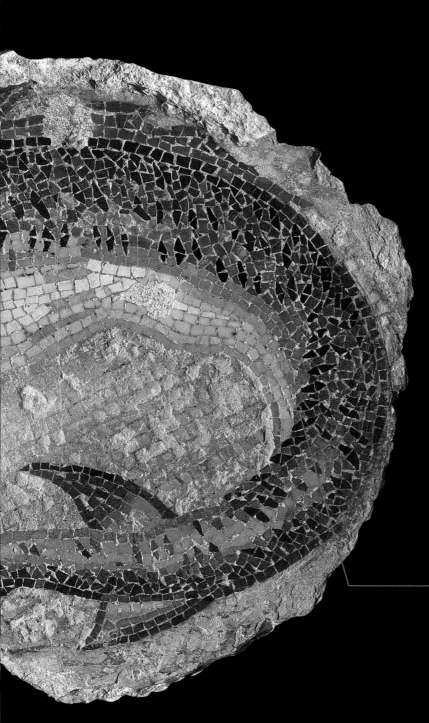

This beautifully detailed, accurate shark picture is part of an ancient Roman mosaic dating from the 1st century CE. The shark's shape shows it is a type of dogfish.

SHARK ATTACKS

One of the biggest myths of all about sharks is that they are terrifyingly dangerous. While a large shark is capable of biting and killing a human, it actually hardly ever happens. What's more, experts think that when sharks do attack us, it's often by mistake.

Jaws is probably the best-known of all shark stories. It started out as a book in 1974 and was made into a movie in 1975. It tells the tale of a huge great white shark terrorizing a holiday island and eating several people. *Jaws* is probably the reason why so many people are especially scared of great white sharks.

Up close
Divers encounter a tiger shark without a problem.

Sharks have been known to bite surfers and their boards. American Bethany Hamilton (left) was bitten by a tiger shark, losing her left arm, while she was paddling a surfboard off Hawaii when she was just 13 years old. She went on to become a professional surfer. Sharks may attack surfers because the surfboard accidentally hits them, or they may think the surfboard is a seal, sea lion, or sea turtle, which are common prey species.

FEAR OF SHARKS

If a shark eats someone, it's reported around the world. We all hear about it, and that makes sharks seem scary and dangerous. But the reason shark attacks make the news is that they are very rare. On average, fewer than 10 people per year, worldwide, die in shark attacks. Many other animals are far more dangerous.

Animal		Human fatalities per year
	Snakes	More than 50,000
	Hippos	More than 2,000
	Crocodiles	About 2,000
	Elephants	About 500
	Bees	More than 100
	Jellyfish	More than 100
	Sharks	Fewer than 10

WHY ATTACKS HAPPEN

Sharks don't normally hunt humans as food. They are more likely to bite if they are provoked, for example by being caught in a net or stepped on, on a coral reef. Certain sharks, such as bull sharks, may attack people fishing in their area. There are also reports of oceanic whitetips eating people stranded in the sea after a shipwreck, especially if they are injured.

Most sharks *wouldn't think that a diver in a wetsuit carrying hard metal oxygen canisters was a tasty meal.*

Of about 450 shark species, most are harmless. Many are too small to have a dangerous bite, while others, such as the basking shark, cannot eat large prey. Mako, hammerhead, reef, lemon, and blue sharks only attack people occasionally. Only four shark species attack more often and are considered dangerous: oceanic whitetips, great whites, bull sharks, and tiger sharks. And even they hardly ever attack!

Oceanic whitetip

Great white shark

Bull shark

Tiger shark

SHARK RELATIVES

Just like humans, sharks have relatives. They belong to a larger fish family, the cartilaginous fish, which also includes rays and skates. Like sharks, these fish all have a flexible cartilage skeleton— though some of them look nothing like their shark cousins!

Spotted eagle ray
This large species of ray measures up to 10 feet (3 m) across.

As rays and skates move slowly and often lie on the seabed, they are at risk of being caught and eaten or trodden on by other animals and humans. To fight back, they have a range of weapons. Skates often have sharp spikes called "bucklers" on their backs. Most rays have a sharp spine on their tails to stab enemies that swim too close. Some rays can even give you an electric shock (see page 66).

The thorny skate has a row of thorns along its back and tail.

FLAT FISH

Rays and skates are like very flat, spread-out sharks. In sharks, the pectoral fins are usually long or pointed, but in rays and skates they are like wide, flat wings joined to the body, head and tail. As most rays and skates use their "wings" for swimming, they don't need strong, upright tail fins. Instead, their tails are long and narrow.

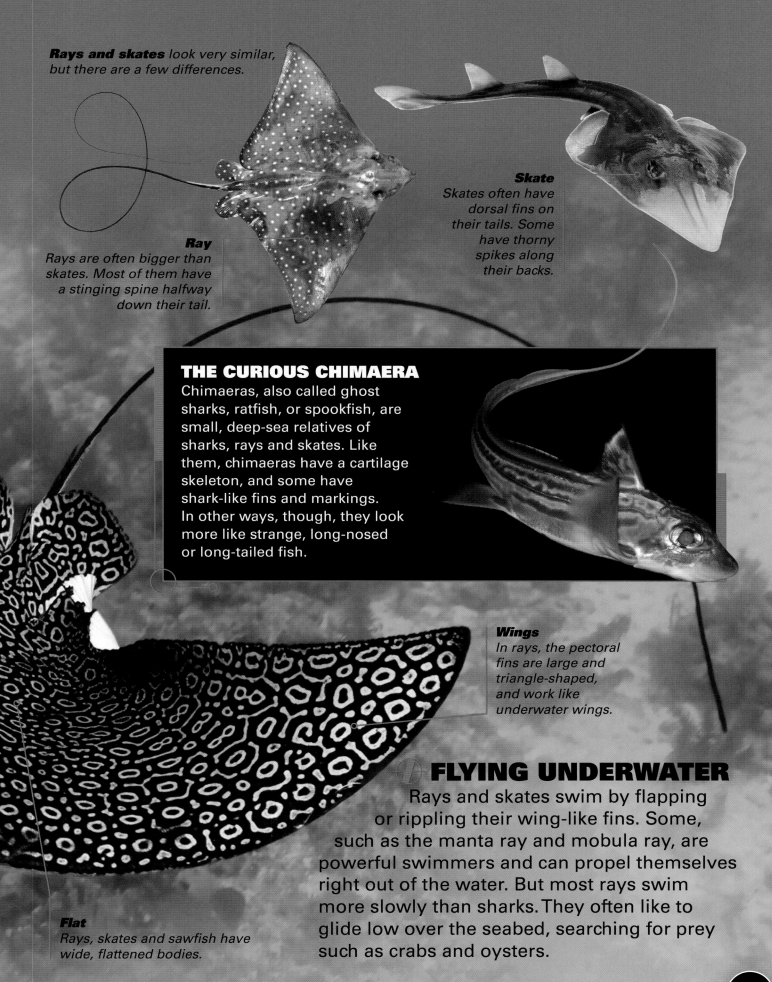

Rays and skates look very similar, but there are a few differences.

Ray
Rays are often bigger than skates. Most of them have a stinging spine halfway down their tail.

Skate
Skates often have dorsal fins on their tails. Some have thorny spikes along their backs.

THE CURIOUS CHIMAERA

Chimaeras, also called ghost sharks, ratfish, or spookfish, are small, deep-sea relatives of sharks, rays and skates. Like them, chimaeras have a cartilage skeleton, and some have shark-like fins and markings. In other ways, though, they look more like strange, long-nosed or long-tailed fish.

Wings
In rays, the pectoral fins are large and triangle-shaped, and work like underwater wings.

FLYING UNDERWATER

Rays and skates swim by flapping or rippling their wing-like fins. Some, such as the manta ray and mobula ray, are powerful swimmers and can propel themselves right out of the water. But most rays swim more slowly than sharks. They often like to glide low over the seabed, searching for prey such as crabs and oysters.

Flat
Rays, skates and sawfish have wide, flattened bodies.

MANTA RAY

Imagine bobbing about in a boat on a calm sea, when suddenly THIS enormous creature, shaped like a spaceship and the size of a large room, leaps up out of the water! It's a shark relative called the giant manta ray, one of the world's biggest fish.

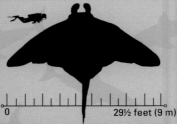
Giant manta ray
This huge ray is hunting for prey in the Caribbean Sea.

BRAINY RAY

The giant manta ray isn't just big, it's also clever. It has the largest brain of any fish, and scientists think it may be a very intelligent animal, like elephants and dolphins. Scientists are trying to work with them to see how they learn and communicate. They often meet up in large groups, and seem to enjoy playing with human divers.

Mouth
Manta rays have big mouths at the front of their snouts.

SPLASH!

When a sea creature this big and wide "breaches," or leaps up out of the sea, it falls back to the surface with a huge belly flop! Manta rays breach a lot, but we aren't sure why they do it. It could be to wash parasites off their skin, or to make a noise to attract other manta rays to the area. Or maybe they just breach for fun—it's hard to tell!

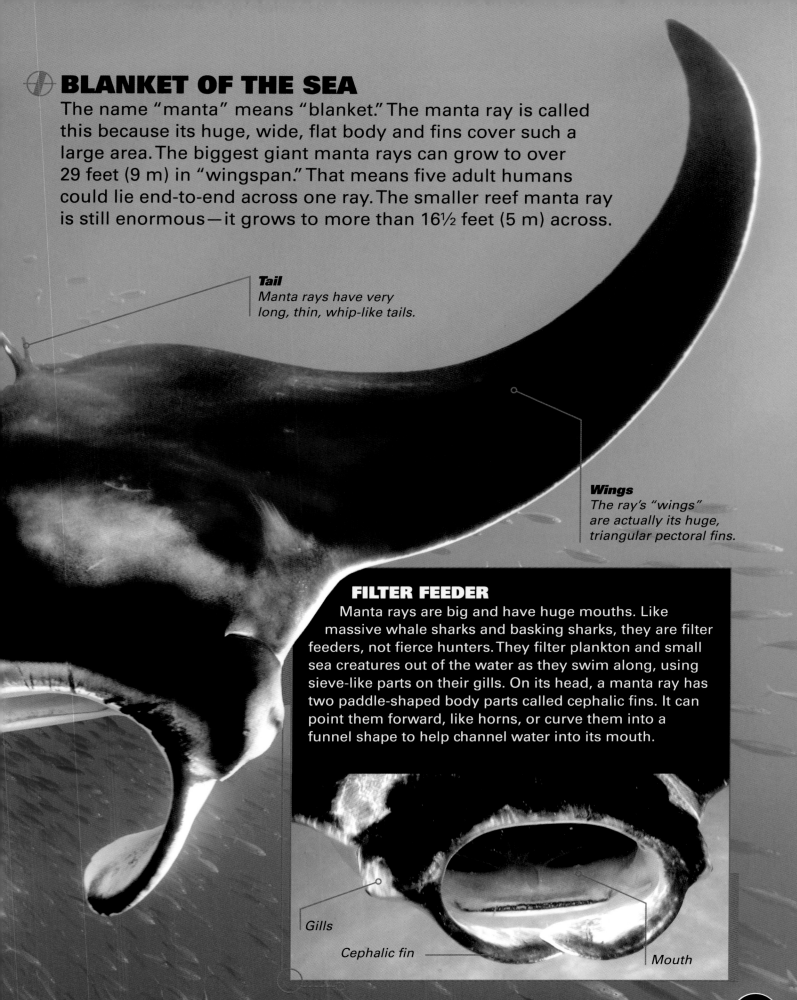

BLANKET OF THE SEA

The name "manta" means "blanket." The manta ray is called this because its huge, wide, flat body and fins cover such a large area. The biggest giant manta rays can grow to over 29 feet (9 m) in "wingspan." That means five adult humans could lie end-to-end across one ray. The smaller reef manta ray is still enormous—it grows to more than 16½ feet (5 m) across.

Tail
Manta rays have very long, thin, whip-like tails.

Wings
The ray's "wings" are actually its huge, triangular pectoral fins.

FILTER FEEDER

Manta rays are big and have huge mouths. Like massive whale sharks and basking sharks, they are filter feeders, not fierce hunters. They filter plankton and small sea creatures out of the water as they swim along, using sieve-like parts on their gills. On its head, a manta ray has two paddle-shaped body parts called cephalic fins. It can point them forward, like horns, or curve them into a funnel shape to help channel water into its mouth.

Gills

Cephalic fin

Mouth

STINGRAYS

Take care! Rays are calm, gentle creatures, but many of them have a stinging spine on their tails. If danger threatens, especially from behind, a stingray will flick its tail up and jab the spine into its enemy with scary speed and force.

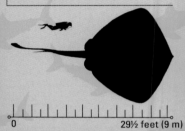
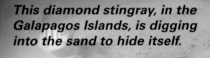

This diamond stingray, in the Galapagos Islands, is digging into the sand to hide itself.

Eyes
This stingray's eyes stick up on top of its head.

DANGER FROM BEHIND

Most stingrays feed by gliding gently over the seabed in search of the small sea creatures that live there. The ray's eyes are on the top of its head and its nostrils and mouth are underneath, so it has to find its food by touch, smell, and its electrical sense. As it snuffles around in the seabed sand, it is at risk of being grabbed from behind by a hungry shark, orca, or other large predator. Its stinging tail helps keep them away.

A close-up view of a stingray's stinging spine.

*A **stingray's stinging spine** is not just a sharp spike. It is usually blade-shaped, with sharp barbs on the sides, so that when it jabs into an enemy's skin it can cause a lot of damage. The spine has a skin-like coating that is soaked in venom. Though not usually deadly to humans, a sting can cause painful cramps—perfect for stopping a predator in its tracks while the stingray escapes.*

Flat and wide
Like all rays and skates, the stingray has a flat body and wide fins or "wings."

Stinging spine
The spine is on the top of the tail. It usually lies flat and points backward.

THE STINGRAY SHUFFLE

Stingrays often hide themselves by lying under a thin layer of sand on the seabed. This means that if you're walking through shallow coastal water, you could easily step on one and get stung. To avoid this, you have to do the "stingray shuffle," sliding your feet forward through the sand. Stingrays can sense the movement and swim away before you reach them.

Seabed dweller
The stingray stays close to the seabed.

ELECTRIC RAYS

All sharks and rays have electroreception—the sixth sense that can detect electricity in the bodies of their prey. But some rays can also give you an electric shock!

FACT FILE

TYPE
Electric rays
(Torpediniformes)

FOUND
Most cool, warm, and tropical seas and oceans, especially coastal and seabed areas

DIET
Small fish, shellfish, crabs, octopuses and other small seabed creatures

0   6 feet (1.8 m)

**SIZE • ½–6 FEET
20 CM–1.8 M**

Eyes
Electric rays have small eyes, and a few species are blind.

ELECTRIC DEFENSE

Electric shocks are very useful for scaring off larger animals that would like to prey on the ray. Large electric rays, such as the Atlantic torpedo ray, can give a shock of up to 220 volts—as strong as the shock from an electric socket—which is enough to stun and paralyze a human and to scare off ocean

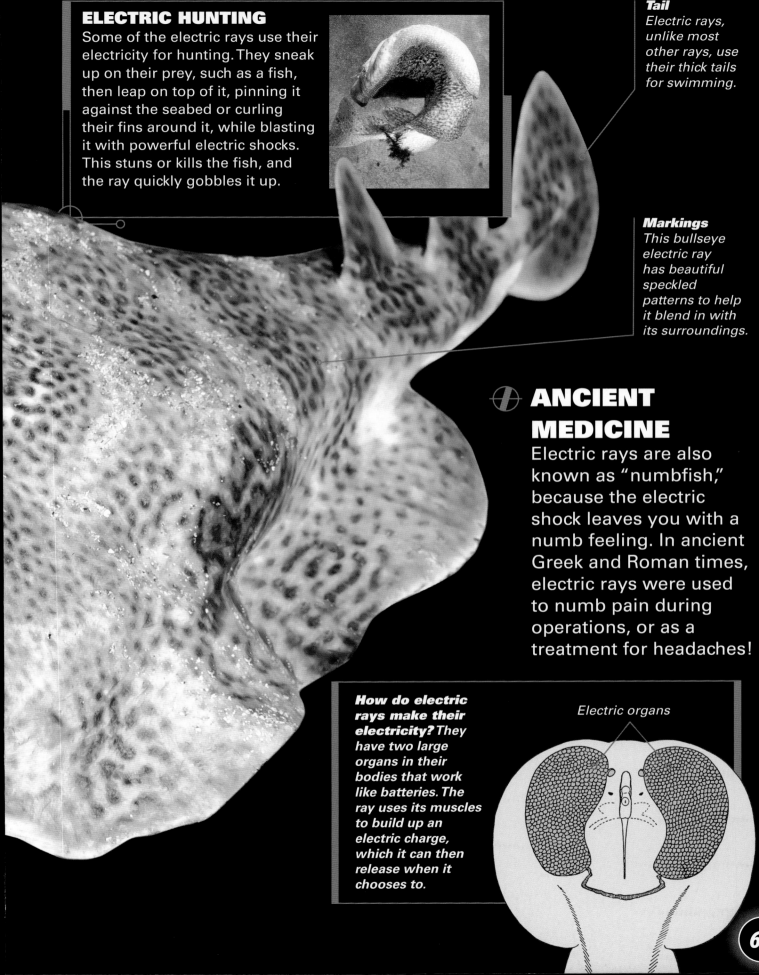

ELECTRIC HUNTING

Some of the electric rays use their electricity for hunting. They sneak up on their prey, such as a fish, then leap on top of it, pinning it against the seabed or curling their fins around it, while blasting it with powerful electric shocks. This stuns or kills the fish, and the ray quickly gobbles it up.

Tail
Electric rays, unlike most other rays, use their thick tails for swimming.

Markings
This bullseye electric ray has beautiful speckled patterns to help it blend in with its surroundings.

ANCIENT MEDICINE

Electric rays are also known as "numbfish," because the electric shock leaves you with a numb feeling. In ancient Greek and Roman times, electric rays were used to numb pain during operations, or as a treatment for headaches!

How do electric rays make their electricity? They have two large organs in their bodies that work like batteries. The ray uses its muscles to build up an electric charge, which it can then release when it chooses to.

Electric organs

SAWFISH

What would it be like to have a 3-foot-long (1 m), sharp-toothed saw for a nose? That's life for the sawfish, a type of ray with an incredibly long, saw-like snout. For a long time, scientists weren't sure how sawfish used their saws, but now we know.

WHAT IS THE SAW FOR?

Until recently, people thought the sawfish mainly used its saw for digging out prey buried in the seabed sand. Then, in 2011, scientists filmed sawfish hunting by slashing the saw from side to side. The sawfish were able to slice and kill fish that were swimming past, or chop up dead fish to make them easier to eat. Sawfish also sweep their saws through a shoal of smaller fish, stabbing several of them to make a meal. The saw is covered in electric sensors that help the sawfish to find its prey.

FACT FILE

TYPE
*Sawfish
(Pristidae)*

FOUND
*Warm and tropical shallow
seas near coasts, and in
some estuaries, rivers
and lakes*

DIET
*Fish and crustaceans, such
as crabs and shrimp*

0   23 feet (7 m)

**SIZE • 3–23 FEET
(1–7 M)**

Shark shaped
*Sawfish aren't as
wide and flat as
other rays, and look
more like sharks.*

Flat bottom
*Unlike most sharks,
sawfish have very
flat undersides.*

SAWFISH IN TROUBLE

Sadly, sawfishes' saws have led to them becoming endangered. Sawfish can accidentally get caught in fishing nets when their saws get entangled. For a long time people have also hunted sawfish for their saws, which are kept as trophies or sold as souvenirs.

Saw
The flat, wide saw, or rostrum, has sharp, tooth-like spikes along both sides.

Mouth
The mouth and nostrils are on the sawfish's underside, as in other types of rays.

SAWFISH AND SAWSHARKS

Sawfish belong to the ray family, but there is also a type of shark that has a saw-shaped snout, which can be confusing! Sawsharks are smaller than sawfish, and their snouts are more pointed. In a sawshark, the teeth around the snout fall out and grow again, but in sawfish, they keep growing throughout the fish's life.

To tell the difference between a sawfish (a type of ray) and a sawshark (a type of shark) at a glance, look out for these telltale signs:

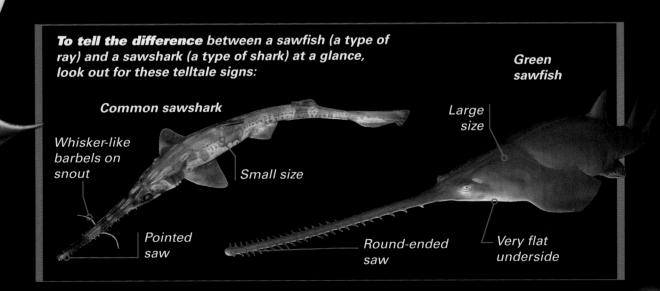

Green sawfish

Common sawshark

Whisker-like barbels on snout

Large size

Small size

Pointed saw

Round-ended saw

Very flat underside

PREHISTORIC SHARKS

When you think of a prehistoric creature, you probably think of a dinosaur. But sharks existed long before dinosaurs did! The first prehistoric sharks lived more than 400 million years ago. When dinosaurs died out, sharks survived in the oceans and lived on.

SHARK FOSSILS

Although prehistoric sharks were very common, whole shark fossils are rare. That's because, being made of soft cartilage, a shark's skeleton rots away quite fast, usually before a fossil can form. Instead, we mostly find fossilized shark teeth, denticles, spines, and harder parts of the shark skeleton, such as pieces of jaw or skull.

MONSTER SHARKS

Not all prehistoric sharks were big, but some were mighty monsters. Megalodon, a fierce hunting shark, was even bigger than a whale shark, the biggest shark alive today. Megalodon had to compete for food with other fierce hunters, such as the prehistoric whale Leviathan.

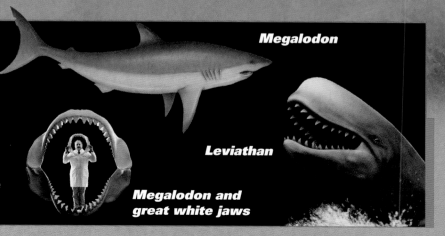

Megalodon

Leviathan

Megalodon and great white jaws

70

Fins
Orthacanthus sharks had long fins running the length of their bodies.

This bizarre shark, Stethacanthus, lived about 350 million years ago. It was about 2 feet (60 cm) long and looked unlike any present-day shark. Stethacanthus had one patch of spiky, tooth-like parts on its head, and another on a wide plate on top of its dorsal fin. No one is sure what they were for.

Orthacanthus
This rare complete shark fossil belongs to a group of sharks named Orthacanthus. They lived from 400 to 225 million years ago and grew to about 10 feet (3 m) long.

Hunter
Like modern sharks, Orthacanthus would have eaten fish.

The teeth of the shark Helicoprion Bessonowi resembled a circular saw.

DETECTIVE WORK

Even when they don't have a complete shark fossil, paleontologists (fossil scientists) can find out a lot from just a few remains. By studying fossil teeth, for example, they can see what type of present-day sharks a prehistoric shark was related to, and figure out its size. They can also tell when a prehistoric shark lived from the age of the rock that the fossil was found in.

SHARKS IN DANGER

Many people think of sharks as fierce and scary creatures, so it might seem odd that they are in trouble. But many species of sharks are endangered and at risk of dying out, for a number of different reasons.

 ## PROBLEMS FOR SHARKS

Here are some of the things humans do that harm and endanger sharks:

• **Shark fishing** People catch sharks for their meat, fins, or skin, and sometimes also for sport.

• **Sea fishing** Sharks often get caught by accident in nets meant for other fish.

• **Destroying habitats** Sharks can die if their coral reef or mangrove forest homes are destroyed.

• **Dropping litter** Some sharks die after swallowing trash that people have dumped in the ocean.

• **Using beach nets** Some beaches have nets around them to keep sharks out, and the sharks can get stuck in the nets.

• **Shark culls** In some places, people kill sharks to try to keep tourist beaches free of them.

More than 100 types of sharks—about a quarter of all shark species—are known to be at risk. Here are some of the most endangered:

Angel shark
Gets caught for food and accidentally in seabed trawling nets. Its habitat is also endangered by seaside tourist resorts.

Daggernose shark
Gets caught in fishing nets and is very endangered as it is only found in a small area off Brazil.

Smalltooth sawfish
Hunted for its fins, meat, skin, and unusual saw. Its muddy estuary habitats are also damaged by development and boating.

WHY SHARKS MATTER

It's important to save shark species, and not just because they are beautiful, fascinating wild animals—although they are! Sharks are also an important part of ocean ecosystems—the finely balanced relationships between living things. For example, tiger sharks feed on turtles, which eat sea grass. Without tiger sharks, there would be too many turtles and they would eat all the sea grass, destroying an important habitat and food source for other species.

WHAT CAN WE DO?

To try to save sharks, governments around the world are now starting to ban fishing for some species, and trading in shark fins and body parts. Some tourist resorts protect local sharks because they can make money from ecotourism—taking tourists to see sharks living in the wild. Understanding sharks helps too; for example, surfers can avoid certain areas or times of day so they don't bump into sharks, reducing any danger.

Trapped
This thresher shark has been accidentally caught in a fishing net and cannot escape.

SHARK SIZES

See at a glance how big (or tiny!) the sharks and rays in this book are compared to each other—and to you!

Human
5½ feet (1.7 m)

Blacktip reef shark
5 feet (1.5 m)

Great white shark
16½ feet (5 m)

Great hammerhead shark
15 feet (4.5 m)

Bull shark
10 feet (3 m)

Shortfin mako shark
10 feet (3 m)

Greenland shark
16½ feet (5 m)

Cookiecutter shark
1½ feet (0.5 m)

Goblin shark
10 feet (3 m)

Frilled shark
5 feet (1.5 m)

Spotted wobbegong shark
8 feet (2.5 m)

Whale shark
39½ feet (12 m)

Megamouth shark
16½ feet (5 m)

Giant manta ray
23 feet (7 m)
(wingspan)

Lemon shark
8 feet (2.5 m)

Atlantic torpedo ray
5 feet (1.5 m)

Blue shark
10 feet (3 m)

Spiny dogfish
3 feet (1 m)

Tiger shark
13 feet (4 m)

Smalltooth sawfish
19½ feet (6 m)

Common thresher shark
16½ feet (5 m)

GLOSSARY

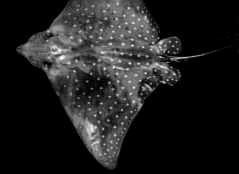

AMPULLAE OF LORENZINI
Holes in the skin of a shark's snout, used to detect electricity.

BARBELS
Finger-like parts around a shark's mouth, used to sense the surroundings.

BIOLUMINESCENT
Living things, including many sharks, that produce a glowing light are bioluminescent.

BONY FISH
Fish—such as trout, carp and tuna—that have a skeleton made of bone.

BREACH
To leap right up out of the water and splash back down.

BUCKLERS
Thorn-like spikes found on the backs of some types of skates.

BUMP
When sharks bump, they push or hit against a person or animal with their snouts.

CARNIVORES
Creatures that eat other animals.

CARTILAGE
Rubbery, flexible substance that sharks' skeletons are made of.

CARTILAGINOUS FISH
Fish that have a skeleton made of cartilage.

CEPHALIC FINS
Horn-like fins found on the heads of some types of rays, such as manta rays.

COLD-BLOODED
Having a body temperature that is controlled by the surroundings, rather than heating or cooling itself.

CORAL
Seashell-like material formed by tiny sea animals called coral polyps as a kind of skeleton.

COUNTERSHADING
Dark coloring above and pale coloring underneath that helps to camouflage an animal when light shines on it from above.

DERMAL DENTICLES
The sharp, tooth-like scales on a shark's skin.

DORSAL FIN
The fin that sticks up in the middle of a shark's back.

ELECTRORECEPTION
An extra sense that sharks have that lets them detect electricity in the bodies of prey animals.

FILTER FEEDER
A shark or other animal that filters or sieves small prey out of the water.

GILLS
Organs that fish use to extract oxygen from the water, so that they can breathe.

GILL SLITS
Openings over the gills, found in sharks and their relatives, that let water flow out.

LAGOONS
Saltwater lakes next to the coast, filled with water from the ocean.

LATERAL LINE
A pressure-sensitive line running along each side of a fish's body.

NICTITATING MEMBRANE
Eyelid-like covers that sharks can close over their eyes to protect them, especially when attacking.

OVIPAROUS
Having babies by laying eggs.

PALEONTOLOGISTS
Scientists who study fossils to find out about prehistoric life.

PARASITE
Living thing that lives on or in the body of another living thing, and takes food from it.

PECTORAL FINS
The two large fins at the lower front end of a shark's body.

PELAGIC
Belonging to the open ocean, away from the coast.

PLACENTA
An organ found in some types of animals that helps to feed babies as they grow inside their mothers.

PLANKTON
A variety of small plants and animals found drifting in water that provide food for many other creatures.

PREDATOR
An animal that hunts and eats other animals.

PREHISTORIC
Events that happened in the time before written history.

PREY
An animal that is hunted and eaten by another living thing.

REEF
A structure on the seabed that often lies just under the water's surface. Reefs can be made of rock, sand or coral, built by coral polyps.

SERRATED
A serrated blade or tooth has a row of sharp points along its edge, making it better at cutting.

SPYHOPPING
When sharks spyhop, they stick their heads out of the water to look around.

UMBILICAL CORD
A cord that connects a baby growing inside its mother to the placenta.

VIVIPAROUS
Giving birth to live babies, instead of laying eggs.

WINGSPAN
The measurement from the tip of one wing to the tip of the other.

INDEX

ampullae of
    Lorenzini 34, 35
angel sharks 72
art, sharks in 56
Atlantic torpedo
    rays 66, 75
attacks 6, 8, 29,
    58–59

baby sharks
    (pups) 44, 45,
    46–47
bamboo sharks 45
barbels 36, 37, 69
basking sharks 8,
    51, 59
beliefs about
    sharks 57
bigeye thresher
    sharks 20, 21
bioluminescence
    39
blacktip reef
    sharks 6, 54,
    55, 74
blue sharks
    18–19, 59, 75
body parts 6
bonnethead
    sharks 11
bony fish 7, 22, 23
brains 29, 35, 62
bramble sharks 24
breaching 9, 17,
    62
breathing 7
bullseye electric
    rays 67

bull sharks 12–13,
    59, 74

camouflage 19,
    26, 28, 36, 37,
    39, 46
captivity 28
Caribbean reef
    sharks 54
carpet sharks 36,
    49
cartilage 7, 22, 23,
    60, 70
cartilaginous fish
    7, 22, 60
cephalic fins 63
chimaeras 61
cleaner fish 29, 55
cold-blooded
    sharks 21
cookiecutter
    sharks 40–41, 74
coral reefs 54
countershading
    19

daggernose
    sharks 72
denticles 24, 25
diamond
    stingrays 64
dogfish 25, 39,
    43, 57, 75
dolphins 7, 40
dorsal fins 6, 10,
    21, 61
dwarf
    lanternsharks
    39

ears 32
egg cases 44, 45
eggs 44–45
electric rays
    66–67
electric shocks
    60, 66–67
electroreception
    11, 34–35, 66, 68
endangered
    sharks 19, 72–73
evolution 7
eyes 11, 17, 20, 32,
    38, 42, 43, 66

filter feeders 8,
    49, 51, 63
fins 6, 10, 16, 18,
    21, 23, 37, 43, 60,
    61, 63, 65, 71
fishing 72, 73
fossils 14, 30, 70,
    71
fresh water 12
frilled sharks
    52–53, 74

gills 6, 7, 49, 51,
    53, 63
goblin sharks
    30–31, 74
gray reef sharks
    54, 55
gray sharks see
    Greenland
    sharks
great
    hammerhead
    sharks 10–11, 74

great white
    sharks 7, 8–9,
    14, 21, 34, 40, 46,
    47, 58, 59, 74
Greenland sharks
    42–43, 74
green
    lanternsharks
    39
green sawfish 69
ground sharks 7
groups, living in 9,
    28, 29, 55

habitat
    destruction 72,
    73
hákarl 42
hammerhead
    sharks 7, 10–11,
    34, 46, 59, 74
hearing 32
horn sharks 45

jaws 22, 31, 70
Jaws (film) 58

lanternsharks
    38–39
lateral lines 33
lemon sharks
    28–29, 34, 47,
    59, 75
lifespan 9
living fossils 30,
    52
longfin mako
    sharks 16, 17

mackerel sharks 7
mako sharks
    16—17, 21, 46,
    59, 74
manta rays 61,
    62—63, 75
Megalodon 14, 70
megamouth
    sharks 50—51, 75
mermaid's purses
    44
mobula rays 61
mouths 7, 11, 21,
    27, 48, 51, 62, 63

network
    wobbegong
    sharks 37
nictitating
    membrane 32
northern
    wobbegong
    sharks 37
nostrils 11, 33
nurse sharks
    15, 36

ocean
    ecosystems 73
oceanic whitetip
    sharks 59
orcas (killer
    whales) 27
Orthacanthus 71
oviparous sharks
    44

pale catsharks 39
parasites 29, 43,
    54, 55, 62
pectoral fins 6, 16,
    18, 21, 60, 61, 63
pelagic sharks 16

pelagic thresher
    sharks 20, 21
photophores 39
placenta 47
prehistoric sharks
    14, 30, 70—71
problems for
    sharks 10, 72

rays 7, 10, 11, 22,
    45, 60—61,
    62—69, 75
reef sharks 6,
    54—55, 59, 74
relatives of
    sharks 60—61

sand tiger sharks
    14, 15, 23, 46
sawfish 68—69,
    72, 75
sawsharks 69
scalloped
    hammerhead
    sharks 11
senses 11, 32—35
shagreen 24
shark fin soup 19
shark gods 56, 57
shark meat 42
shortfin mako
    sharks 16, 17, 74
sizes 74—75
skates 22, 60—61
skeletons 7,
    22—23, 60, 70
skin 24—25
sleeper sharks 43
small-spotted
    catsharks 44
smalltooth
    sawfish
    72, 75

smell, sense of 33
smooth
    hammerhead
    sharks 11
snouts 6, 31, 33,
    34, 38, 68, 69
species of shark 7
spined pygmy
    sharks 39
spotted
    wobbegong
    sharks 37, 74
spyhopping 9
Stethacanthus 71
stinging spines
    60, 61, 64, 65
"stingray shuffle"
    65
stingrays 64—65
swell sharks 44
swimming speeds
    17

tails 6, 7, 20, 23,
    30, 50, 67
tasseled
    wobbegong
    sharks 37
taste, sense of 33
teeth 9, 14—15, 31,
    38, 41, 51, 52, 71
thorny skates 60
threat displays 55
thresher sharks
    20—21, 73, 75
tiger sharks 7, 14,
    23, 26—27, 46,
    58, 59, 73, 75

touch, sense of 33

urea 42

velvet belly
    lanternsharks
    38, 39
vertical migration
    41
vision 11, 17, 27,
    28, 32, 38, 42, 43
viviparous sharks
    46

warm-blooded
    sharks 21
whale sharks 8,
    36, 47, 48—49,
    50, 57, 74
whitetip reef
    sharks 54, 55
wobbegong
    sharks 36—37,
    49, 74

zebra sharks 36,
    45, 46, 49

ACKNOWLEDGMENTS

Picture credits

(t=top, b=bottom, l=left, r=right, c=center, FC=front cover, BC=back cover)

Alamy Stock Photo BC (fin) © Mark Conlin, 1b © Martin Strmiska, 2/3 © Wolfgang Pölzer, 11bc © WILDLIFE GmbH, 20bl © Roberto Nistri, 22/23 © Michael Wheatley, 26cr © Andre Seale, 27br © Brandon Cole Marine Photography, 45tc © FLPA, 45tr © Mark Conlin, 45br © Mark Conlin, 56tr © david hancock, 60/61 © imageBROKER, 60bl © blickwinkel, 66/67 © Marli Wakeling, 70bl © Stocktrek Images, Inc., 70br © Stocktrek Images, Inc., 72tr © Arco Images GmbH, 74 (greenland shark) © Roberto Nistri.

© Andy Murch/Elasmodiver.com 8/9, 48/49, 62cl, 69br

Corbis 4tr © Louie Psihoyos, 13tr © Guiziou Franck/Hemis, 20/21 © Ian Coleman (WAC)/Nature Picture, 22bl © 68/Ocean, 29tr © Jeffrey L. Rotman, 32/33 © Stephen Frink/Science Faction, 34/35 © Scubazoo/SuperStock, 36/37 © Fred Bavendam/Minden Pictures, 44tr a) © Ingo Arndt/Minden Pictures, 44tr b) © Flip Nicklin/Minden Pictures, 51bc © Wild Wonders of Europe / Sá/Nature Picture, 58bl © Splash News, 61cr © Wild Wonders of Europe / Lundgren/Nature, 64cl © Pete Oxford/Minden Pictures, 64/65 © Paul Souders, 70bl © Louie Psihoyos, 71br © Colin Keates/Dorling Kindersley Ltd., 72/73 © Jeffrey Rotman, 73tr © Luciano Candisani/Minden Pictures, 75 (Atlantic torpedo ray) © Fred Bavendam/Minden Pictures.

FLPA 65br Luciano Candisani/Minden Pictures/FLPA

Fotolibra 20cr Miles Kelly Publishing, 33br Miles Kelly Publishing, 70bc Miles Kelly Publishing.

Getty Images 1t © Jim Abernethy, 12/13 © ullstein bild / Contributor, 21b Dorling Kindersley, 24cl DEA / A. DAGLI ORTI / Contributor, 25cr Doug Perrine, 27tr Education Images / Contributor, 28tl Brian J. Skerry, 33tr Franco Banfi, 37br Daniela Dirscherl, 40/41 Bill Curtsinger, 42cl Adam Seward/ NIS, 47tr Brian J. Skerry, 51br Dorling Kindersley, 52/53 Getty Images / Staff, 53tl Getty Images / Staff, 54/55 Alexander Safonov, 55tl Reinhard Dirscherl, 56/57 Mondadori Portfolio / Contributor, 58/59 Jim Abernethy, 59bl (whitetip) Jim Abernethy, 59br (tiger) Jim Abernethy, 62/63 Westend61, 69tl Underwood Archives / Contributor, 74 (cookiecutter) Dorling Kindersley -Thinkstock, 74 (frilled shark) Getty Images / Staff, 75 (megamouth) Dorling Kindersley.

© Ken Sutherland 28/29

Nature Picture Library 9br Chris & Monique Fallows, 10/11 © David Fleetham, 11bl © Ian Coleman (WAC), 16br Ian Coleman (WAC), 24/25 Alex Hyde, 26/27 Alex Mustard, 44/45 Robert Thompson, 46tr Alex Mustard, 46/47 Doug Perrine, 50/51 Bruce Rasner/ Rotman, 52cl Solvin Zankl, 74 (shortfin mako) Ian Coleman (WAC), 74 (spotted wobbegong) Alex Mustard.

© OceanwideImages.com 28br, 63br, 67t, 68/69, 69bl

Photoshot 51tr © Photoshot, 58tr © Photoshot/Collection Christophel, 72br (smalltooth sawfish) © NHPA/Photoshot, 75 (smalltooth sawfish) © NHPA/Photoshot.

Science Photo Library FC Andy Murch/Visuals Unlimited, Inc., BC (eye) Scubazoo, 14bcl Richard Bizley, 25tr Pascal Goetgheluck, 35tr Jacopin// BSIP, 65tr David Fleetham, Visuals Unlimited, 71tr Jaime Chirinos.

SeaPics 5b © Wolfgang Poelzer/SeaPics.com, 16bl © Rodrigo Friscione/SeaPics.com, 16/17 © Masa Ushioda/SeaPics.com, 17tr © Richard Ellis/ SeaPics.com, 18/19 © Wolfgang Poelzer/SeaPics.com, 20br © Jason Arnold/SeaPics.com, 32br © Jeff Rotman/SeaPics.com, 37tr © Nigel Marsh/ SeaPics.com, 38/39 © Espen Rekdal/SeaPics.com, 40bl © Michael S. Nolan/SeaPics.com, 42/43 © Saul Gonor/SeaPics.com, 43tr © George W. Benz/ SeaPics.com, 45tl © Nigel Marsh/SeaPics.com, 74 (goblin shark) © e-Photo/Makoto Hirose/SeaPics.com.

Shutterstock FC bl Rich Carey, BCtl Matt9122, BC (tooth) BW Folsom, 6bl Eric Isselee, 6/7 Andrea Izzotti, 7tr cbpix, 7cr Neirfy, 11tr © Matt9122, 11br © IrinaK, 12br © Cobus Olivier, 13tr (inset) © Rainer Lesniewski, 14cl © Photon75, 14bl (great white) © Triduza Studio, 14bcr BW Folsom, 14br Ryan M. Bolton, 14/15 MP cz, 15br nicolas.voisin44, 16/17 (background) Deep OV, 19bc 54613, 23bl photowind, 23br Blamb, 34cl © Fiona Ayerst, 39br IrinaK, 41tr Egorov Artem, 48bl Ethan Daniels, 49tl Dudarev Mikhail, 50br Triduza Studio, 57br Joanne Weston, 59bl (great white) Jim Agronick, 59br (bull shark) Shane Gross, 61tl fluke samed, 61tr Nataliya Taratunina, 74 (diver) ostill, 74 (blacktip) Eric Isselee, 74 (great white) Triduza Studio, 74 (great hammerhead) Matt9122, 74 (bull shark) Shane Gross, 74 (whale shark) kaschibo, 75 (lemon shark) Yann hubert, 75 (manta ray) Triduza Studio, 75 (blue shark) Pommeyrol Vincent, 75 (spiny dogfish) IrinaK, 75 (tiger shark) Luiz Felipe V. Puntel, 75 (thresher) nicolas.voisin44, 76t fluke samed, 78 © IrinaK, 79 Dray van Beeck.

Topfoto 9tr © National Pictures/TopFoto, 30/31 © Photoshot/TopFoto

Victoria Museum, Australia 31br

Other Wikipedia: 19tl (public domain), 30b Citron / CC-BY-SA-3.0), 56bl dustinpsmith CC BY 2.0 (http://creativecommons.org/licenses/by/2.0/ legalcode), 67br (public domain), 70/71 (public domain), 72cr (public domain)